A Parent's Guide to

DOWN SYNDROME

A Parent's Guide to

DOWN SYNDROME

Toward A Brighter Future

by

Siegfried M. Pueschel, M.D., Ph.D., M.P.H.
Professor of Pediatrics
Brown University
and
Director
Child Development Center
Rhode Island Hospital
Providence, Rhode Island
with invited contributors

·P·A·U·L·H·
BROOKES
PUBLISHING CO.

Baltimore • London • Toronto • Sydney

Paul H. Brookes Publishing Co.
P.O. Box 10624
Baltimore, Maryland 21285-0624

www.brookespublishing.com

Typeset by Brushwood Graphics, Inc., Baltimore, Maryland.
Manufactured in the United States of America by
The Maple Press Company, York, Pennsylvania.

Fourth printing, July 1995.
Fifth printing, April 1999.

Library of Congress Cataloging-in-Publication Data

Pueschel, Siegfried M.
    A parent's guide to Down syndrome: toward a brighter future / by
Siegfried M. Pueschel.
        p.   cm.
    Includes bibliographical references.
    ISBN 1-55766-060-3
    1. Down's syndrome—Popular works.   I. Title.
RJ506.D68P832   1990
616.85'8842—dc20   90-1527
                                                                  CIP

Contents

98650

About the Authors

Siegfried M. Pueschel, M.D., Ph.D., M.P.H., studied medicine in Germany and graduated from the Medical Academy of Düsseldorf with an M.D. degree in 1960. He then pursued his postgraduate studies at The Children's Hospital in Boston, Massachusetts, and the Montreal Children's Hospital in Quebec, Canada. In 1967 he earned a Master of Public Health degree from the Harvard School of Public Health, and in 1985 he was awarded a Ph.D. degree in Developmental Psychology from the University of Rhode Island. From 1967 to 1975 Dr. Pueschel worked at the Developmental Evaluation Clinic of The Children's Hospital in Boston. There he became director of the first Down Syndrome Program and provided leadership to the PKU and Inborn Errors of Metabolism Program. In 1975 Dr. Pueschel was appointed director of the Child Development Center at Rhode Island Hospital in Providence, Rhode Island. He continued to pursue his interest in clinical activities, research, and teaching in the fields of development disabilities, biochemical genetics, and chromosome abnormalities. Dr. Pueschel is certified by the American Board of Pediatrics and is a Diplomate of the American Board of Medical Genetics. His academic appointments include Lecturer in Pediatrics, Harvard Medical School, and Professor of Pediatrics, Brown University. Dr. Pueschel has published extensively in the medical literature. He has authored or co-authored 10 books and has written over 150 scientific articles relating to many types of handicapping conditions. Available through Paul H. Brookes Publishing Co. are *The Special Child: A Source Book for Parents of Children with Developmental Disabilities, The Young Person with Down Syndrome: Transition from Adolescence to Adulthood, New Perspectives on Down Syndrome*, and *Prevention of Developmental Disabilities*. Dr. Pueschel is the proud father of Chris, who has Down syndrome.

Claire D. Canning, B.A.,
a concerned parent, received
her Bachelor of Arts degree
from Newton College of the
Sacred Heart. She is the
mother of five children. Because the birth of her last child,
Martha, with Down syndrome
was such a moving experience,
she has spent much of her time
trying to ameliorate this experience for others. She is the

author of *The Gift of Martha,* and a co-author of *Down Syndrome: Growing
and Learning.* Together with her husband, she continues to be a community activist for persons with mental retardation. They live in Ports-
mouth, Rhode Island.

Ann Murphy, M.S.W.,
is the Director of Social Ser-
vice, Developmental Evaluation
Clinic, The Children's Hospital,
Boston. She is also an Adjunct
Assistant Professor at the Bos-
ton University School of Social
Work. She is a co-author of
*Down Syndrome: Growing and
Learning.* She was a co-inves-
tigator in a study funded by the
National Institutes of Health on

Down syndrome during the early 1970s.

Elizabeth   Zausmer,
M.Ed., P.T., was the director of
training in physical therapy at
the Developmental Evaluation
Clinic at Children's Hospital
Medical Center in Boston, an
adjunct assistant professor at
Boston University's Sargent
College of Allied Health Pro-
fessions, and a lecturer at Sim-
mons College in Boston. At the
present time, she is a Senior

Advisor in Child Development at the Developmental Evaluation Clinic
of The Children's Hospital in Boston. She is a co-author of *Down Syndrome: Growing and Learning.*

Jean P. Edwards, D.S.W.,
has taught at Portland State
University in Portland, Oregon, for 22 years. She has
directed numerous research
projects related to issues of adolescent transition and adult
life for persons with disabilities. She is known for her work
with community integration
and has directed a number of
successful job placement and

community living programs. She is a professor and an adjunct faculty
member at Oregon Health Sciences University and directs the Social/
Sexual Training Project for persons with disabilities. She is the author of
numerous books including *My Friend David,* a sourcebook on Down
syndrome.

Bud Fredericks, Ed.D.,
is a research professor with
Teaching Research, Western
Oregon State College. He is the
parent of Timothy, a young
man with Down syndrome.
His research interests over the
years have kept pace with the
age of his son. Many years ago
he focused upon early intervention matters, developing
models for early intervention

programs that were adopted nationally. He has developed curriculum
used at the preschool and elementary levels. Most recently he has de-
voted his energies to the establishment of residential facilities for those
with the most challenging behaviors and has attempted to provide for
that same population meaningful community-based employment opportunities utilizing the supported employment model. In addition, he
has developed vocational models for those at the transition level with
moderate and severe disabilities. A secondary area of research is on
those who are severely emotionally disturbed, a population for which
he has established residential classroom and vocational models in addition to parent training approaches for adolescents with severe challenging behavioral difficulties. However, throughout all of his research his
primary focus has been the education of children with Down syndrome.

DeAnna Horstmeier, **Ph.D.,** is presently a lecturer in Special Education at The Ohio State University. She has administered the university early intervention program and served as the parent language training coordinator. She has authored various chapters and books on language training, including *Ready, Set, Go: Talk to Me* for parents and therapists. Her primary qualification is having the joy and challenge of being the mother of Scott Allen, a youth with Down syndrome.

Scott W. Weaver, **B.S.,** is the Director of Training and Games for Colorado Special Olympics. He has been involved with Special Olympics since 1982 as a coach, trainer, event director, sports director, and program coordinator. He received his Bachelor's degree in Parks and Recreation, with an emphasis in Recreational Therapy, from Slippery Rock University of Pennsylvania. For 4 years, Scott was Director of Recreation and Leisure Services for the North Shore (Massachusetts) Association for Retarded Citizens. Scott is a frequent speaker and enjoys cycling, tennis, skiing, and coaching.

Foreword

In the short span of years since this book was first published in 1978, outstanding progress has been made to create better life chances for persons with Down syndrome. Progress has been particularly impressive in terms of the public's improved perception of this chromosome disorder. The authors of this book have been at the cutting edge of these advances through their teaching, their contributions to the professional literature, and above all, their extensive clinical and personal contacts over many years with families having a member with Down syndrome. Noteworthy in this updated edition is the new material on educational programming, on language development, and on the sexual awakening of the adolescent.

As we wrote in the foreword to the previous edition, *Down Syndrome: Growing and Learning*, this is a book not about a syndrome, but about children. These children have chromosomes that happen to be arranged in special ways, and the arrangement is referred to as Down syndrome. We have found that if the emphasis is put on the syndrome, it can appear that these children are very much alike, and that they constitute a clearly defined "category." But if the syndrome is pushed into the background so that the children are liberated from this category and regarded as individuals, it is clear that they differ quite markedly from one another, and that, indeed, they are more similar to the average child in the community in the ways they grow and develop than they are different.

In reading this book we are reminded of the many families we have come to know in different countries who have a child with Down syndrome. How much their lives would be enriched, how much their child's physical and social well-being would be improved, if only they could have access to the information Dr. Pueschel and his co-authors offer in this volume. Of course, it is not just a matter of information; every page here reflects a respectful attitude and a warm feeling toward all children with handicaps and specifically toward those with Down syndrome, the latter of whom for so long have been labeled and libeled as ineducable and incompetent "Mongoloids." The "self-fulfilling prophecy" of these children's supposed deficiencies has kept them excluded from many helpful programs and activities.

A Parent's Guide to Down Syndrome: Toward A Brighter Future takes another step away from the frustrations of the past by providing families, professional workers, and volunteers with detailed, readily understood guidance to further the physical, social, mental, and emotional development of the child with Down syndrome, with special emphasis given to early intervention. As the authors themselves state, the overriding purpose of this book is to convey to parents that there is hope, that a child with Down syndrome is first and foremost a human being with all of humanity's inherent strengths and weaknesses, and that we do see a brighter future for our children.

For professional workers as well as for families, the teamwork that produced this book should have more than symbolic meaning. It clearly demonstrates that success will depend on positive interaction between us and all.

Rosemary Dybwad, Ph.D.
Gunnar Dybwad, Ph.D.
Heller School
Brandeis University
Waltham, MA

Acknowledgments

I first want to express my gratitude to the many children with Down syndrome I have been privileged to serve over the past decades. These extraordinary children have taught me much that I in turn may teach others.

I would also like to thank the many parents who provided us with photographs of their beautiful children, who bring life to many chapters of this book.

I also would like to express my gratitude to Melissa A. Behm of Paul H. Brookes Publishing Company, for her ready accessibility to discuss matters pertaining to editing and publishing this volume and for her assistance and guidance.

Last but not least, I am indebted to Jill Rose, who single-handedly prepared the manuscript. Beyond her outstanding secretarial skills, she put her heart into this book.

Siegfried M. Pueschel

Introduction

During the past decade significant progress has occurred in the field of Down syndrome. Scientific advances in both the biomedical and the behavioral sciences, in addition to attitudinal changes in society, have necessitated a revision and expansion of *Down Syndrome: Growing and Learning* (Pueschel, Canning, Murphy, & Zausmer, 1978). Whereas some chapters of that book required only minor changes and updating for inclusion here, others were completely rewritten. Moreover, several new chapters were added, incorporating new knowledge and accomplishments in the field that update this volume to the 1990s and beyond. The book's primary purpose remains the same: to provide state-of-the-art information that should enhance the quality of all aspects of life for persons with Down syndrome.

In addition to the four previous authors (Claire D. Canning, Ann Murphy, Siegfried M. Pueschel, and Elizabeth Zausmer), four new authors (Jean P. Edwards, H.D. Bud Fredericks, DeAnna Horstmeier, and Scott Weaver) contribute expertise in specific areas. Although most of the authors are highly qualified professionals in their respective disciplines who have contributed significantly to progress in Down syndrome, it is noteworthy that four of the authors are also parents of children with Down syndrome. Their personal experience in raising a child with special needs and their innate concern and interest in improving the quality of life of individuals with Down syndrome add a special dimension to this book.

This book is written primarily for parents of children with Down syndrome, as well as for others who want to learn more about the subject. Although not intended to be a textbook for instructional purposes, the volume will undoubtedly also be educational for students and professionals. Nevertheless, whether our readers are parents, friends of parents, students, or professional workers in the field, this book will afford them a greater understanding of Down syndrome.

In addition to discussing general aspects of Down syndrome, this book attempts to portray an accurate and positive picture of the person with Down syndrome from birth to adulthood. Clearly, this book cannot offer an encyclopedic treatment of every aspect of life for these individuals. Rather, our main goal is to provide a general overview, highlighting important developmental stages in the life of the person with Down syndrome and emphasizing the accomplishments of the past and present, while preparing for the challenges of the future.

REFERENCE

Pueschel, S.M., Canning, C.D., Murphy, A., & Zausmer, E. (1978). *Down syndrome: Growing and learning.* Kansas City: Andrews, McMeel & Parker.

To
Chris, Martha,
Timothy, and Scott Allen

From Parent to Parent

Claire D. Canning

As we approach the twenty-first century, human expectations for the quality of life are higher than ever before. Our hopes and dreams still soar at the impending birth of a new baby. Yet when we are told our baby has Down syndrome and we must reshape our hopes and dreams, I believe the original parental sorrows remain the same.

Of all the joys and sorrows of a lifetime of living, no event in our lives was ever more traumatic for my husband and me than the birth of Martha, our daughter who has Down syndrome. We were shocked, shattered, bewildered. No woman ever really expects to give birth to a defective child. Prior to Martha's birth, mental retardation had been simply a statistic to us, something that happens to someone else. Yet no child has ever taught *us* so much.

If you are the parent of an older child with Down syndrome, you have probably already formed a special bond with other parents of children with special needs, parents who have shared the same intense joys and sorrows. If you are in special education or a related professional field, you, too, must be elated at the progress that has occurred in mental retardation and human services. Your continued encouragement and reinforcement and your willingness to see each child as a unique and valuable human being can add immeasurable dimensions to the life of the child with special needs and to his or her family.

If you are a new parent, I can share the deep sorrow you feel in every fiber of your being, the aching disappointment, the hurt pride, the terrible fear of the unknown. But I can tell you from personal experience that having known this ultimate sorrow, you will soon learn to cope better with every phase of life. You *will* be happy once again, and through your child you will receive undreamed of love, joy, and satisfaction.

Life cannot remain the same. The decisions to choose a profession or a new career, to marry, or to have a child—all important milestones in our lives—imply change. The addition to a family of a child with Down syndrome precipitates even more rapid change, but the loving support you will meet at each phase will be an enriching experience.

My first fear was for our marriage. If it had been a shaky commitment, the new child could have provided us with an opportunity to blame each other or to make excuses for never finding time for self, for each other, or friends. But if you work at it, this special child can be the

opportunity for better communication, for finding new courage and love in your partner. Personally, I have never appreciated my husband so much; the feeling of mutual support has enhanced our marriage.

I feared for our other four children. I wanted to give them enough time so that they would not feel neglected or harbor unspoken feelings of shame or resentment. Their response, their potential for love, has overwhelmed us. They have given us courage in so many ways, and in turn they have not been cheated, but enriched. Together, we have all learned the dignity and worth of each human being.

I feared so for our new little child, Martha. This was surely not the life I had intended to give her. But I have learned that her life is very precious, that she is singularly happy and loves unquestioningly with a degree that makes me wonder just what constitutes "normality." She has truly been a joy to us.

Compared to the bleak future that formerly awaited the child with mental retardation, these last two decades have seen remarkable progress for the child with special needs, perhaps more progress than in the 100 years preceding. The public in general is experiencing a new awareness and compassion. New programs and services are mandated by law to guide and support us and our children from birth to adulthood, and we as parents must work to ensure their continuation.

After an initial period of trauma following Martha's birth, we were very fortunate to join a marvelous program for children with Down syndrome, run by professionals whose expertise and love and respect for every human being guided us through our most difficult days. Fortunately, similar human services and guidance programs to assist you in planning for your child's development now exist all over the country. The professionals in our program during

Martha's early years became far more than advisers to us: they are friends to whom we will always be grateful.

One of the gifts that Martha's birth brought us has been a wonderful network of friendships with other parents. These parents have successfully combined their own careers with the loving care of special children. We would never have had the opportunity to know these friends without Martha. They have unflinchingly worked against what we once felt to be great odds. Their courage has uplifted us and caused us to look more realistically at life's true values. Lifelong friendships have become even richer as our friends seem to share a special pride in Martha's accomplishments. I like to think that the entire community has profited. Their kindness and compassion have overwhelmed us.

As for Martha herself, how do I think of her today as a teenager and young adult? She is a constant source of joy in our lives. She is placid and gentle, but has a quiet enthusiasm and gratitude for the simplest favor. She laughs easily and often, and her courage and happiness teach me so much about life's true values. She willingly assumes responsibility for homework and chores, and delights in being a young adult. She attends our local public high school, where she is enrolled in a special class but is mainstreamed as much as possible within her capabilities. We feel so fortunate that she has a marvelously dedicated teacher and aide and enthusiastic teachers for her mainstreamed classes. We have been continually uplifted by the school's positive learning atmosphere and the community support we have received from other teachers and her high school peers. Thanks to PL 94-142, the federal law that mandates and guarantees the education of all children with handicaps from ages 3 to 21, Martha will remain in school and combine academics with job training for the future until graduation.

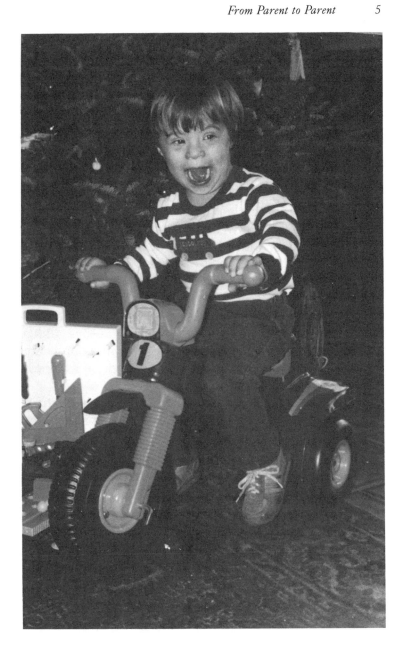

If your child is young, you will soon learn that the child with Down syndrome does almost everything a normal child does, but more slowly. With love and understanding, our children can achieve many things once unexpected of them. They will walk, and run, and laugh, and tell you when they are thirsty or hungry. They usually will be able to read and write, will love school and music, and will delight in travel. They will swim, bowl, take ballet lessons, join Boy Scouts or Girl Scouts, take sailing, horseback riding, and piano lessons, go to camp, make First Communion, Confirmation, or Bar Mitzvah, among so many other things we might wish for all our children. They will respond well to gentle discipline. They will have a definite sense of humor, a great sense of the ridiculous, and will learn much from socialization and imitation. Their sensitivity will even console us if we are sad. They will be bundles of mischief, imps with sticky fingers, and, only incidentally, children who happen to have handicaps. Unlike our other children, they will love us unconditionally and unquestioningly, with a resolve and tenacity that almost defies understanding.

What do we as parents wish for Martha in the future? I think the most valuable thing we can give her is complete

acceptance of her just as she is, and a desire to make her as independent as possible for the future. From the community, I ask for compassion, but not pity, and the chance for her to prove herself as fully as possible while being accorded all the rights of a human being within her capabilities. Our greatest hope is that some day when we are no longer here, she may live in a carefully supervised setting within the community, overseen by her siblings, where she may know the joys of friendship, the dignity of self-worth, and the usefulness of work in a protected atmosphere.

As parents, we have learned that there is little more we can wish for any of our children, but that they develop their potential to the best of their abilities. In the end, all the material accomplishments of this world won't matter much at all. What will endure is the quality of love we have given each other. For us, what seemed like the tragedy of our lives has become our greatest and most fulfilling opportunity. Indeed, we have been richly blessed.

A Child with Down Syndrome Is Born

Ann Murphy

The birth of a child is a momentous event in a family's life. The parents have spent 9 months imagining what the baby will be like and what effect he or she will have on the family. New relationships, roles, and responsibilities have been envisioned to provide for the child's care and also to meet the family's social and economic needs. Simultaneously, practical arrangements have been made regarding care, clothing, space, and furnishings. Relatives, friends, and co-workers have focused attention on the expectant parents, and the anticipated birth has become a major topic of conversation. During the pregnancy, many parents might voice concern that something might go wrong, but this is usually fleeting and is brushed aside, particularly if there have been no problems with the pregnancy and no family member has a handicap.

LEARNING THAT YOU
HAVE A HANDICAPPED CHILD

Then the day finally arrives: The child is born. Will the parents realize their expectations?

If the newborn has a handicap, the parents may be quickly aware that something is not quite right. They notice a tenseness and anxiety in the staff attending the delivery or in others involved in caring for them and the baby immediately afterward. The nurses seem subdued.

The physician explains that there are concerns about the baby's condition. Perhaps the parents themselves have noticed something different about the child's appearance. They are afraid. Then the doctor informs them that their child has Down syndrome. The words may be unfamiliar and mean little except that they are associated with mental retardation.

All parents who have experienced this moment describe sensations of overwhelming shock and disbelief, as though the world were coming to an end. They find it hard to listen further to the doctor's comments, so absorbed are they in the feelings and images people have about mental retardation and Down syndrome. They may think of individuals who are clumsy and have difficulty communicating; who look different, with large misshapen heads; who lack the potential to react like others; and who cannot recognize family members or respond to them with love and affection. (These stereotypical perceptions are common across all levels of education and intelligence.) Most parents furthermore express fear and a desire to escape from the situation. One parent said, "I was like a little kid. I wanted to say 'take it away, take it back,' but I knew it wouldn't go away."

Some people try to escape the overwhelming reality by hoping some mistake has been made, that the chromosome test will prove the doctor wrong and that their child will be an exception. At the same time, the parents may feel guilty for having such thoughts. However, these are very natural reactions to a crisis and reflect the need of all human beings to try to escape a seemingly untenable situation. Some couples have difficulty communicating with one another about their new baby's diagnosis. Their styles of managing stress may differ, as well as their previous experience with and values regarding handicapping conditions. These differences may make it hard for them to share questions, concerns, and information. This is a time when parents are sensitive about their personal adequacy and are prone to feeling blamed and devalued by the reactions of others.

When parents are told that Down syndrome occurs once in every 800 to 1,100 births, they cannot help but brood about why it happened to them. Most people seek an explanation within their own personal behavior or those close to them. They search for something that happened that may have been overlooked. They may blame themselves or others. It is sometimes easier to blame a person or a specific event for one's painful feelings, rather than relating them to statistical abstractions. As just mentioned, many parents fear that having such a child reflects in some way on their own competence and that other people may think less of them if they have given birth to a mentally retarded child.

People handle their feelings in different ways: some by withdrawing into themselves, others by expressing their feelings openly by crying or getting angry. Some people actively seek information, ask questions, and make telephone calls, whereas others wait for people around them to volunteer their reactions and ideas. It takes most people months to regain a sense of their usual self and to get in touch with their normal routines and attachments. Their feelings of sadness and loss may never disappear completely, but many people describe some beneficial effects of such an experience. They feel that they gain a new perspective on the meaning of life and a sensitivity to what is truly important. Sometimes a shattering experience such as this can strengthen and unify a family.

GETTING TO KNOW THE BABY

Many parents acknowledge a reluctance to get close to the baby. At first, some are afraid to look because they fear the

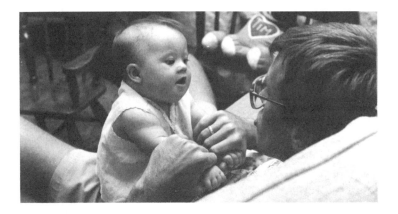

baby may have an odd or unusual appearance. Others are timid about having physical contact with the child. They feel that somehow by touching, they are claiming the child as their own and committing themselves to assuming responsibility for his or her future. Some parents are uncertain about accepting a child with a disability into their family life, investing their feelings in a person who may bring sadness rather than pleasure. However, once the parents overcome their inhibitions and actually begin to look at the baby and to touch, hold, and care for him or her, they are often impressed with the fact that the child is, after all, a baby and in most ways resembles other babies more than differs from them. The opportunity to have contact with the child can enhance the feeling of normalcy. As with any new baby, most parental energy is channeled into learning his or her individual characteristics. Parents may soon be so impressed with the child's relatively normal appearance and behavior that they find it hard to believe there is anything wrong. Some parents describe endless hours inspecting and observing the baby, trying to capture his or her "differentness."

The period of time involved in becoming reasonably comfortable with the child varies from family to family. On hearing the diagnosis, some parents experience a strong protective urge. Others continue to be uncertain and unsure about their feelings for months. A few are really unable to relate to a child with a handicap. One parent described the process of acceptance in the following way: "First I realized what she would never be, then I learned what she did not have to be, and finally I think I have come to terms with what she is and can be." Such feelings of sadness and loss are apt to be revived when parents are feeling down or when special occasions remind them of what normal children can accomplish that their child with Down syndrome cannot.

LEARNING ABOUT DOWN SYNDROME

As just indicated, most parents need considerable time, often weeks and months, to come to terms with this new child mentally, to decide whether they can love him or her as they feel parents should, and to determine whether they will be able to provide the child with the special care that may be required. During this time, they try to predict what a future with the child will be like, what problems will emerge, and how they might cope in the years to come. They try to compress all of the future into the present because they have no guidelines to draw upon to give them security in this new relationship and to aid in their decision making. They need opportunities to express their feelings and to ask questions, as well as access to accurate information.

The professional staff in many maternity hospitals are grappling with the same feelings and concerns of parents. Their work allows them little contact with handicapped children, current philosophies, or new programs. Often their ideas are conditioned by their own early experiences rather than up-to-date knowledge and information. Some doctors feel uncomfortable and pessimistic about children with mental retardation, because there is no specific cure that can be offered to the family. These individuals may be unaware of how much can be accomplished through education and training and that most communities provide programs for children of all ages who have mental retardation. At the same time, many doctors and other health practitioners offer empathy, understanding, support, and knowledgeable guidance to families of children with Down syndrome.

INFORMING OTHER PEOPLE

Once parents are convinced that their child has Down syndrome, they are often unsure whether to tell other people or of the appropriate timing for doing so. Some families

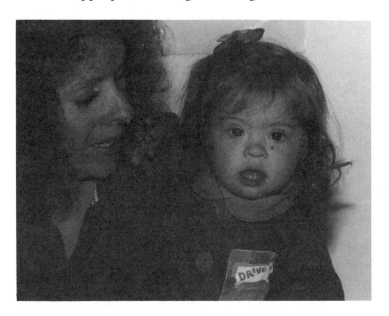

question whether it might not be better to keep it a secret until they have become more used to it themselves. Others feel that if other people know, it may prevent them from treating the child normally. Nevertheless, many people will notice that there is something different about the child's appearance or else will be aware of the parents' tension and sadness. They may thus be reluctant to initiate conversation regarding the baby, with the result that awkwardness in relationships develops between the parents and close relatives and friends.

The desire to postpone informing relatives and close friends may indicate that the parents have not really accepted the child's handicap. However, talking about the child's condition, although it reopens the wound, in some ways confirms that what happened is real, rather than a dream. Although painful, talking with other people about the child's condition can be an important step in working through sadness and shock, and in regaining former confidence and personal equilibrium.

Often relatives and friends are concerned about what role they should play when they hear that the baby has a disability. They are fearful that their overtures will be interpreted as either an intrusion or a curiosity. They will welcome some clue that their presence is desired and that their support and interest will be considered helpful. Sometimes communications break down when parents are waiting for some proof that people close to them still care. It is usually wise to proceed with the normal routine followed by the hospital and community after the birth of the baby, such as having the child's picture taken and listing the birth in the community newspaper. These are activities that are ordinarily planned. They can also help parents feel more like their usual selves.

Grandparents may need some extra assistance during this time. Often their knowledge of children with handicaps may be derived from previous experiences. They may be especially concerned about the implications for their adult children and preoccupied with how the parents can be protected from stress. They may find it more difficult to listen to the parents' perspective and to allow them to develop their own resolution of the issues. The opportunity to talk with the involved professional people may help them focus their concerns appropriately.

TALKING WITH THE CHILD'S SISTERS AND BROTHERS

Most parents are uncertain about what they should say to their other children. It is natural to want to protect them from the worries of adults. Parents may also be embarrassed to talk with their children or feel guilty that somehow they have compromised their future by giving them a sister or brother with mental retardation. Some parents underestimate the sensitivity of their children to their parents' feelings or their ability to note differences in the baby's appearance and developmental course. Experience has shown that it is important to talk with the other children as soon as possible.

Children of different ages will have different concerns. Young children will sense a parent's mood. They will probably not be aware of the actual differences in the baby until they notice that he or she does not walk as soon as the brother or sister of a friend. Older children will note differences in appearance, as will their friends. When asked about their sibling, they will feel more comfortable if they have been given information and an explanation that they can offer. They will also be interested in knowing what caused the condition and what can be done "to fix it." Adolescents may be concerned about whether they will be more likely than the average person to reproduce a handicapped child. All ages can gain by accompanying their sibling on visits to the pediatrician or to the early intervention program. The younger children can benefit by not feeling left out, in addition to learning something from the activities in the doctor's office or early intervention program. School-age children and adolescents may have questions they want to discuss with professionals. They should be encouraged to ask such questions, and time should be set aside for this purpose. Some centers have programs specifically designed to provide information to brothers and sisters of children with handicaps.

Raising a Child with a Handicap

Ann Murphy

P arents who are raising a child with a handicap increasingly have available to them the supports they need to help their children achieve their maximum potential. The objective is to provide the resources and opportunities afforded to parents of normal children, but at the same time to give supplementary assistance to alleviate the extra demands of caring for a child with a handicap. In the past, parents of children with handicaps did not have access to the many information sources accessible to parents of normal children. Now, professionals in a variety of fields have more positive attitudes toward children with disabilities and are able to focus on the children's strengths and assets as well as limitations. In addition, there is increased recognition of the resources that are needed to support families in this new challenge.

LEARNING ABOUT DOWN SYNDROME

An important first step is to learn about what Down syndrome is. People use different resources to obtain information. Family members and friends may not be the best

sources of information, as they, like the parents, may associate Down syndrome with still-prevalent stereotypes. A pediatrician with special training in developmental disabilities can be a reliable resource. He or she can examine the child and provide perspective about how the child relates to the larger population of children with this diagnosis.

There is also a growing and varied body of literature about Down syndrome. Some literature focuses on the adjustment of the family, whereas other literature emphasizes the development of the child. It is important to check the date of publication, as older literature may be irrelevant or inaccurate. The best literature about the development of individuals with Down syndrome is apt to concentrate on young children. Professionals are still learning

about the long-range potential and outcomes. Only in recent decades have children with this diagnosis had the benefit of early stimulation, community-based education, and social opportunities.

Parents of other young children with Down syndrome are also a valuable resource. Parents who have recognized the value of this type of contact have organized parent groups in various parts of the country and have made themselves available for consultation. Usually the helping parents have undergone a period of training as to what their role should be. It is often comforting and reassuring for parents to learn that many other people have had thoughts and feelings similar to theirs. They can also share information about the daily care of their child and about what adjustments they have had to make. (Parents are often surprised to learn that most children with Down syndrome function like other children in many ways.) Other parents can also provide helpful information about local opportunities in the community that may be difficult to glean from books, directories, or professionals. Names of "resource parents" can sometimes be obtained from the staff of the maternity hospitals, the pediatrician, or a local parent group. It may be useful to talk with more than one family, because each person's values, life-style, and experiences differ. Parents should not be concerned about asking direct questions or requesting to see the child of the resource parents. However, parents should not allow other people to tell them how they should feel or what is the right direction for them.

No matter how comprehensive the search for information, there will still be many unanswered questions about what the future will hold for the child and how the family will cope. The most important thing at this stage is for the parents to get some ideas about what the next few months may be like and to locate resources in their local community.

SUPPORT SERVICES FOR THE CHILD'S DEVELOPMENT

All parents, particularly new parents of children with handicaps, need a reliable professional resource in their community that is available to them for ongoing questions and special concerns. Even very experienced parents feel this need with a child who has a developmental disability. They are not always sure how much of their previous knowledge applies, and they need someone to help them sort this out. An important source of such support is a qualified pediatrician who is interested and knowledgeable regarding the development of children with handicaps. Some pediatricians are more oriented toward the diagnosis and treatment of specific diseases and are less qualified to help parents assess their child's developmental progress. In the pediatrician's office the parents will have plenty of opportunities to learn in what ways their child differs from other children, but if this is the principal focus of every visit, the parents do not gain much of a perspective about how parent and child should work together. Thus, periodic contact with a pediatrician who specializes in children with developmental disabilities can be an important adjunct to routine pediatric care. Such specialized pediatricians see many children with Down syndrome on a regular basis and they keep abreast of knowledge about the development of these children. Such physicians may be located in child development programs of university-based teaching hospitals. Often they also may have access to specialists from other disciplines, such as nutrition, psychology, nursing, and social work, who can provide consultations in a number of developmental areas.

Increasingly, specialists in the development of children with handicaps are finding that early guided management of the child's development may make a significant difference in his or her later functioning. There are many different opinions as to how and why this is helpful. Some studies stress that the most significant impact of early intervention programs is on the parents' morale, since the programs offer parents a continuing relationship with someone who has a positive interest in their child. This contact, in turn, is thought to help them function more normally in their relationship with their child. Other studies stress that guidance from such programs assists parents in identifying indicators of the child's readiness to move forward developmentally and that it provides technical knowledge that enhances the child's potential to act on this readiness. Thus, there is a focus on prevention of secondary handicaps. Still others emphasize that this early guided stimulation brings the child more in contact with his or her surroundings and accelerates learning and achievements. No one claims that such programs will cure a disability, but most parents who have had this kind of support and encouragement feel that it is of immeasurable value in raising their child. The professionals who staff such programs are from a variety of disciplines, including early childhood education, social work, nursing, physical therapy, occupational therapy, psychology, and speech therapy. Often they work in teams and make contact with families through home visits or at local centers.

Sometimes these developmental specialists work with children and families in small groups. The content of programs typically includes techniques of working with the child, information about local services, emotional support and guidance, and parent discussion groups. Such programs are now available in most states. Although often operated by private agencies, they are sponsored and supported by divisions of the state government such as a department of public health, education, or mental retardation. They usually are available for families whose children range in age from newborns to age 3. The costs of such services are often reimbursable through a combination of health insurance and public funds. The federal government has increasingly recognized the value of such programs by encouraging states, through financial incentives, to develop and extend the availability of early intervention for all families who have a child with a developmental disability.

PLANNING FOR SCHOOL AND WORK

The modern philosophy of normalization has greatly influenced educational and recreational programming for children with handicaps. This means that whenever possible the child with a disability should participate in activities and opportunities available to nonhandicapped children who are his or her age peers. Increasingly, parents have a variety of options from which to choose, the decision being based on the individual needs of the child. School systems are required by federal laws PL 94-142 and PL 99-457, as well as state laws, to develop appropriate educational pro-

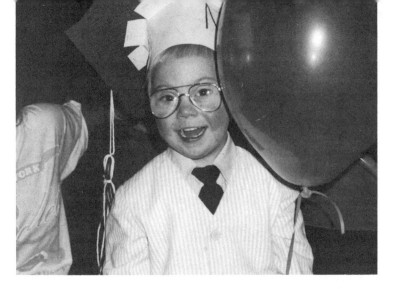

grams for children with handicaps in the least restrictive environment. There are no developmental or health prerequisites for a school program. Often public schools have a range of educational programs for preschool-age children with handicaps, beginning at age 3 and sometimes even for infants. If the child has been enrolled in an early intervention program, there is often a transition process in which staff from both systems are involved in making the appropriate plan. The schools are also required to reevaluate the child's learning needs and to develop an individualized education program (IEP), which often includes remedial help in such developmental areas as motor skills and language. The parents should be actively involved in the evaluation process. They are also entitled to monitor the program and to ask for revisions if indicated. If there are disagreements between the school and parents that cannot be resolved, there is a written appeal process.

Some parents question whether their child should attend a regular class rather than a program for children with special needs. There is considerable debate among professionals and parents about the role of special education and about how children best learn. However, each family should decide with the help of professional consultation what is best for their child. Children with Down syndrome differ widely in their communication, motor development, socialization, and self-help skills. The child's needs should be matched with available programs. The philosophy of the school and community, as well as the skills of the involved professionals, will also be important factors in making decisions about the child's school plans. All children with handicaps should have opportunities to interact with their "normal" age peers, either in school, in the neighborhood, or in community activity groups. This is beneficial to both the child with a disability as well as to "normal" children.

Currently children with educational handicaps may remain in the public school system until age 22, so long as they can benefit from this extended education. There may be a gradual deemphasis on academic subjects and an increased focus on skill development to prepare them for employment and independent living. It is important that the parents' expectations be such that the parents work to prepare the child within the home for these roles as well. Like other children, children with handicaps need to learn to take responsibility for themselves and to accommodate to the needs of others.

Once high school is completed, the state Division of Rehabilitation and/or Division of Mental Retardation has a responsibility to guide young people with handicaps toward educational and training opportunities suited to their potential. Often there is public funding for the tuition and transportation to the recommended programs.

RECREATIONAL OPTIONS

Many communities have organized separate social and group experiences for children and adults with retardation. These may be sponsored by the public school, parents' associations, or the municipal park and recreation de-

partment. Organizations specializing in recreation such as the Boy Scouts or YMCA/YWCA increasingly feel some responsibility to include children with handicaps in their recreational programs. Many communities have special swimming programs for persons with handicaps, even providing individualized instruction.

Again, parents must consider whether their child's recreational needs are best served in a special program or in a program that integrates children with disabilities with their age peers. Important factors to consider are the match between the child's social skills, coordination, independence in self-care, interest in the particular activity, and the expectations of the program. Some programs are prepared to individualize the needs of participants and to offer extra support and instruction. In choosing leisure activities, the major goal should be that the child learn something about being a group member and about how to offer support and solicit support from peers, and that the child will have a good time.

FINANCIAL ASSISTANCE

Parents often ask whether particular financial subsidies are available to families raising a child with a handicap. For many families, there are none at present. However, many states are considering providing families of handicapped children with a subsidy for incidental special expenses. Some states have pilot projects in place. Usually, there are some income guidelines as well as specific definitions of eligible handicaps. Families with low incomes may be eligible for Supplemental Security Income, which can be applied for through a local Social Security office. If the child is deemed to have a substantial disability and the family's income level falls within the required range, the child may receive a stipend to assist with living expenses and become eligible for Medicaid, which covers all medical expenses. When the child reaches 18 years of age, the family's income is not considered in determining eligibility for Supplemental Security Income.

Parents sometimes want information about setting up a trust fund for the child's future special needs. In this regard, it is important that they consult a lawyer knowledgeable in this field; otherwise, the funds might be a barrier to eligibility for public resources to which the young adult might be entitled.

RESPITE CARE

Public subsidy of respite care is a concept growing in popularity. Many states have respite care programs, which allow for payment of personnel to assist the family in meeting the needs of the child with a handicap, so that the family can be free to carry out other commitments or to have occasional leisure time. Eligibility requirements and the extent of the service vary, but it involves a caregiver or companion who can assume responsibility for supervising the child for a period of time, sometimes in a center-based program and at other times in the home. The care may be scheduled for short ongoing periods at intervals, or it may involve a block of time while the family takes a vacation.

ADVOCATES

Many states offer technical assistance in locating and establishing eligibility for community programs. State personnel also can advocate for families who are dissatisfied with the quality of response they have received from publicly supported programs. It is wise for parents to become informed about the National Down Syndrome Congress located in Chicago, Illinois, and the Association for Retarded Citizens located in Arlington, Texas. These parent organizations have often provided leadership in developing services. Parents vary in their interest and ability to be active in organized groups, but these organizations can provide vital information about current developments that may be highly relevant to families with a child with Down syndrome.

COMMUNITY-BASED
LIVING AND WORKING

The future for a person with retardation can potentially include the range of options open to "normal" citizens. The current trend is to develop supported living and work situations that can accommodate a broad range of capabilities. Ideally, these are located in the community and designed so that the young person can function as independently as possible. Many individuals with Down syndrome are capable of working in competitive employment. For others, supported employment or sheltered work environments may be more appropriate.

A variety of living situations is potentially available for those who need some assistance. These include condominiums and apartments with some staff on hand who monitor the living arrangement or are available for consultation, as well as closely supervised small-group living situations. However, resources fall short of the need. Therefore, it is important to identify one's needs early and to learn about application procedures as well as the groups who are trying to promote the development of new resources.

GUARDIANSHIP

Parents often wonder about guardianship for a young adult with mental retardation. Any person in our society who reaches the age of 18 years automatically becomes his or her own guardian, unless there are clear indications that the individual is unable to handle his or her own affairs with advice and guidance. If possible, it is preferable that the person be his or her own guardian, to enhance his or her self-esteem and sense of competency. If parents have questions about this, they can arrange for an evaluation of the young adult by a clinical team comprising a physician, social worker, and psychologist to assess the young person's level of adaptive abilities. Sometimes, it is useful to designate a partial guardianship, which may be restricted to specific areas of decision making such as medical care or finances.

COUNSELING AND SPECIAL SERVICES

Most communities have counseling services to help families who are experiencing special problems in caring for their child with a handicap. Family service and child welfare agencies can help families better adjust to the numerous aspects of care or provide technical assistance in areas of concern such as behavior and social functioning.

A Historical Viewpoint

Siegfried M. Pueschel

P arents often wonder whether Down syndrome has been with mankind since early civilization or whether it is a condition that only emerged in recent times. Although there is no definite answer to this question, it must be assumed that throughout biological history and evolution of mankind there have been numerous gene mutations and chromosome changes. Thus, many known genetic diseases and chromosome disorders, including Down syndrome, probably have occurred in previous centuries and millennia.

The earliest anthropological record of Down syndrome probably stems from excavations of a Saxon skull, dating back to the seventh century, that has structural changes often seen in children with Down syndrome. Some people believe that Down syndrome has been sculpturally and pictorially represented in the past. For example, the facial features of figurines sculpted by the Olmec culture nearly 3,000 years ago have been thought to resemble those of persons with Down syndrome. Careful examination of these figurines, however, casts doubt on this assertion.

In an attempt to identify children with Down syndrome in early paintings, Hans Zellweger surmised that the 15th-century artist Andrea Mantegna, who painted several pictures of Madonnas holding Jesus, depicted the infant Jesus with features suggestive of Down syndrome in the painting *Virgin and Child* (Figure 1). Zellweger also

Figure 1.   *Virgin and Child*, by Andrea Mantegna (c. 1430–1506). Tempera on panel, 48.5 cm × 34.6 cm. Courtesy, Museum of Fine Arts, Boston; George Nixon Black Fund.

claimed that an infant with Down syndrome was represented in the painting *Adoration of the Shepherds*, painted by the Flemish artist Jacob Jordaens in 1618. Yet, a critical inspection of the child in this painting does not permit a definite diagnosis of Down syndrome. Similarly, a painting by Sir Joshua Reynolds done in 1773 and titled *Lady Cockburn and Her Children* (Figure 2) contains a child with certain facial characteristics resembling those usually noted in Down syndrome. However, since this child later became Sir George Cockburn, the admiral of the British Fleet, it is highly unlikely that this child had Down syndrome.

Figure 2. *Lady Cockburn and Her Children*, by Sir Joshua Reynolds (1723–1792). Courtesy, Alinari/Art Resource, New York.

Despite the preceding historical conjectures, no well-documented reports of persons with Down syndrome were published prior to the nineteenth century. There are a number of reasons for this: first, there were very few medical journals available then; second, only a few researchers were interested in children with genetic problems and mental retardation; third, other diseases such as infections and malnutrition were prevalent then, overshadowing many of the malformation and genetic problems; and fourth, by the mid-19th century, only half of the mothers survived beyond their 35th birthday (it is well known that there is an increased incidence of Down syndrome in mothers of advanced age), and many children who indeed were born with Down syndrome probably died in early infancy.

The first description of a child who presumably had Down syndrome was provided by Jean Esquirol in 1838. Shortly thereafter, in 1846, Edouard Seguin described a patient with features suggestive of Down syndrome, a condition he called "furfuraceous idiocy." In 1866 Duncan noted a girl "with a small round head, Chinese looking eyes, projecting a large tongue who only knew a few words." That same year, John Langdon Down (Figure 3) published a paper describing some of the characteristics of the syndrome that today bears his name. Down mentioned: "The hair is not black as in the real mongol but of a brownish color straight and scanty. The face is flat and broad. The eyes are obliquely placed. The nose is small. These children have considerable power of imitation."

Down deserves credit for describing some of the classical features of this condition and thus distinguishing these children from others with mental retardation, in particular, those with cretinism (a congenital thyroid disorder). Thus, Down's great contribution was his recognition of the physical characteristics and his description of the condition as a distinct and separate entity.

Figure 3.   John Langdon Down. From *The Practitioner, 210,* 172. © The Marcus Beck Collection, Royal Society of Medicine, England; reprinted with permission.

Along with many other contemporary scientists of the mid-19th century, Down undoubtedly was influenced by Charles Darwin's book, *Origin of Species*. In keeping with Darwin's theory of evolution, Down believed that the condition we now call Down syndrome was a reversion to a primitive racial type. Recognizing a somewhat Oriental appearance in the affected children, Down coined the term "mongolism" and inappropriately call the condition "mongolian idiocy." Today we know that the racial implications are incorrect. For this reason, and also because of the negative ethnic connotation of the terms *mongol*, *mongoloid*, and *mongolism*, such terminology should definitely be avoided. According to some authors, the use of such terminology could jeopardize the potential for social acceptance of these children, justice in allocation of education and other resources, and determination of long-range policy for opportunity. More importantly, to call a child with Down syndrome a mongoloid idiot is not only a demeaning insult to the child but also an incorrect description of the person, who, although having a mental handicap, is first and foremost a human being who is capable of learning and functioning well in society.

After 1866 no reports on Down syndrome were published for about a decade until J. Fraser and A. Mitchell in 1876 described patients with this condition, calling them "Kalmuck idiots." Mitchell drew attention to the shortened head (*brachycephaly*) and to the increased age of the mothers when they gave birth. Fraser and Mitchell deserve credit for providing the first scientific report on Down syndrome, at a meeting in Edinburgh in 1875, when Mitchell presented observations on 62 persons with Down syndrome.

In 1877, William Ireland included patients with Down syndrome as a special type in his book, *Idiocy and Imbecility*. G.E. Shuttleworth stated in 1886 that these children were "unfinished" and that "their peculiar appearance [was] really that of a phase of fetal life." During the latter part of the 19th century, scientists also noted the increased frequency of congenital heart disease in persons with Down syndrome. In 1896 Smith described the hand of a person with Down syndrome, noting the incurved little finger.

At the beginning of this century, many medical reports were published describing additional details of abnormal findings in persons with Down syndrome and discussing various possible causes. Progress in the method of visualizing chromosomes in the mid 1950s allowed more accurate studies of human chromosomes, leading to Lejeune's discovery more than 30 years ago that children with Down syndrome have one extra #21 chromosome.

Thus, during the past decades much has been learned about the chromosome abnormality, genetic concerns, biochemical disorders, and various medical problems relating to Down syndrome. Although many of the mysteries surrounding Down syndrome have been unraveled, there are still many unanswered questions that will require future research to provide us with a better understanding of this disorder.

Cause of Down Syndrome

Siegfried M. Pueschel

When a child with Down syndrome is born, parents often ask "How did it happen? What have I done? Why did it happen?" These and other related questions have been asked over and over again by many parents. Yet, to this point no satisfactory answers to these questions have been found.

Since Down syndrome was first described more than a century ago, medical scientists have searched for answers and proposed many theories for its cause. Both astute observations and misleading concepts have been put forward. In the beginning of the twentieth century, some physicians thought that since the time of bodily maldevelopment of the child with Down syndrome had to be in the early part of pregnancy, that the condition resulted from some environmental influence during the first 2 months of pregnancy. Others more correctly believed that genetic aspects were the cause. Unsupported reports, speculations, and misconceptions often led to untenable conjectures such as that alcoholism, syphilis, tuberculosis, or regression to a primitive human type were causes of Down syndrome. Many other false hypotheses could be mentioned here. Yet, most lacked a strong scientific basis and today seem absurd, considering our present state of knowledge.

By the early 1930s, some physicians suspected that Down syndrome might be due to a chromosome[1] problem. However, at that time techniques for examining chromosomes were not advanced to the point that this theory could be proven. When in 1956 new laboratory methods became available allowing scientists to visualize and study chromosomes, it was found that instead of 48 chromosomes as previously assumed, there were 46 chromosomes in each normal human cell.

Three years later, in 1959, Lejeune reported that the child with Down syndrome had 1 extra small chromosome. In studies of such children, he observed 47 chromosomes in each cell instead of the normal 46, and instead of the ordinary two #21 chromosomes, he found three #21 chromosomes in each cell, which led to the term *trisomy 21*. Subsequently, geneticists detected that, in addition, there were other chromosome problems in children with Down syndrome—namely, *translocation* and *mosaicism*.

It may help to explain these chromosome abnormalities in more detail. There are normally 46 chromosomes in each cell, as seen in Figure 1. These chromosomes are usually arranged in pairs according to size, as depicted in Figures 2 and 3. There are 22 pairs of "regular" chromosomes (autosomes) and two sex chromosomes, which are XX in the female (see Figure 2) and XY in the male (see Figure 3), adding up to 46 chromosomes in each normal cell.

Half of each individual's chromosomes are derived from the father and the other half from the mother. Germ cells (that is, sperm and eggs) only have half the number of

----

[1]Chromosomes are tiny rodlike structures that carry the genes; they are inside the nucleus of each cell and can only be identified during a certain phase of cell division by means of microscopic examination.

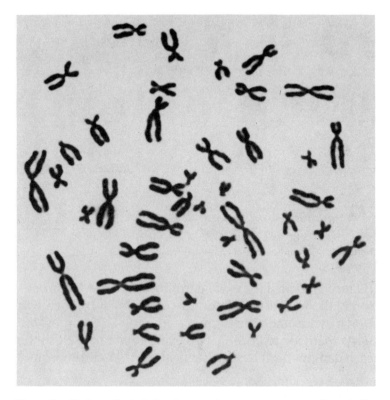

Figure 1.   Photograph depicting human chromosomes as seen through the microscope.

chromosomes ordinarily found in other cells of the body. Hence, 23 chromosomes are in the egg (*ovum*), and 23 chromosomes are in the sperm. Under normal circumstances, when sperm and egg are united at the time of conception, there will be a total of 46 chromosomes in the first cell. Ordinarily, this cell will start to divide and continue to do so as shown in Figure 4.

However, if one germ cell, egg or sperm, has an additional chromosome (that is, 24 chromosomes) and the other germ cell has 23 chromosomes, this will lead at the time of conception to a new cell having 47 chromosomes

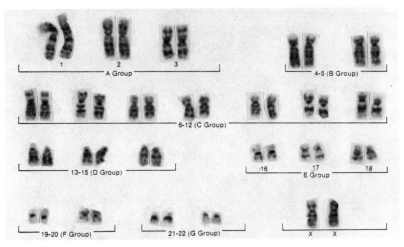

Figure 2.   Chromosomes from a normal female.

(Figure 5). And if the extra chromosome is a #21 chromosome, the individual, if not miscarried, will be born with Down syndrome. The original cell with 47 chromosomes starts to divide to become two exact copies of itself so that each daughter cell has an identical set of 47 chromosomes.

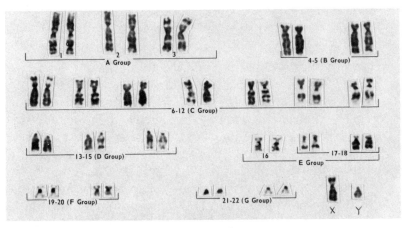

Figure 3.   Chromosomes from a normal male.

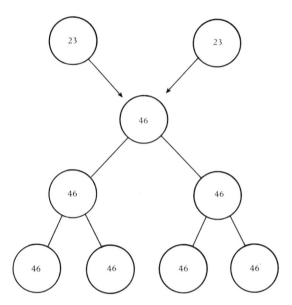

Figure 4. Twenty-three chromosomes derive from each germ cell. At fertilization, the first cell has 46 chromosomes. Under normal circumstances, this cell will continue to divide, and in subsequent cell generations, each cell will have 46 chromosomes.

The process of cell division then continues in this fashion. Later, after delivery, the child's blood cells as well as all other body cells will contain 47 chromosomes, indicating trisomy 21.

As indicated previously in this book, mothers often feel guilty that something they might have done during pregnancy caused the baby to have Down syndrome. However, since, as already explained, the extra #21 chromosome is usually already present in the sperm or egg prior to conception, the abnormality cannot be the mother's fault or the result of anything she did or did not do during pregnancy.

The question is often asked, "How does the extra chromosome get into the cells?" The faulty cell division can occur in one of three places: in the sperm, the egg, or

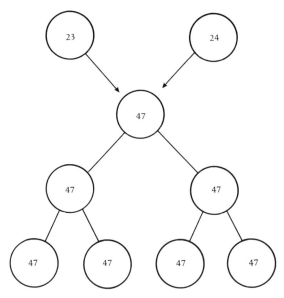

Figure 5. If one of the germ cells (sperm or egg) contributes an extra #21 chromosome, then the first cell will have 47 chromosomes, and (if not miscarried), a child with Down syndrome will be born.

during the first cell division after fertilization; the latter possibility is probably quite rare. It has been estimated that in 20% to 30% of cases, the extra #21 chromosome is the result of a faulty cell division in the sperm (that is, the extra chromosome is derived from the father) and that in 70% to 80% of cases the extra chromosome comes from the mother.

The mechanism of the faulty cell division is thought to be the same in all three situations. As shown in Figure 6, the two #21 chromosomes are somehow "stuck together" and do not separate properly. This process of faulty separation of chromosomes is called "nondisjunction," because the two chromosomes do not "disjoin" or separate as they would ordinarily during normal cell division. Approximately 95% of children with Down syndrome have this form of chromosome abnormality, the earlier-mentioned

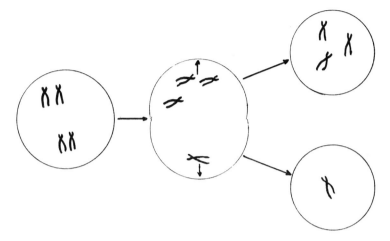

Figure 6. During cell division, two #21 chromosomes "stick together" (non-disjunction). In the following cell generation, one cell will have one chromosome less (this is not a viable cell), and the other cell will have one additional chromosome. (For demonstration purposes, only two pairs of chromosomes are shown here.)

trisomy 21, as depicted in Figure 7. Parents should know that once they have a child with trisomy 21, the chance that a future child may be born with Down syndrome is about 1 in 100.

In another 3% to 4% of children with Down syndrome, there is a somewhat different chromosome problem, called translocation. In children with translocation, the total number of chromosomes in the cells is 46, the extra #21 chromosome is attached to another chromosome, so that again there is a total of three #21 chromosomes present in each cell. The difference in this instance is that the third #21 chromosome is not a "free" chromosome but is attached or translocated to another chromosome, usually a #14, #21, or #22 chromosome; however, the extra #21 chromosome or part thereof could also be attached to other chromosomes. In Figure 8, the extra #21 chromosome is shown translocated to a #14 chromosome.

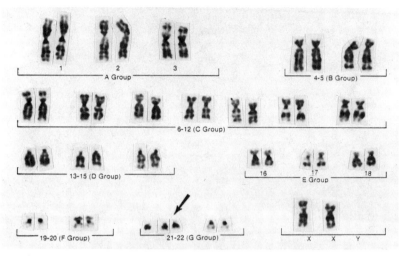

Figure 7. Chromosomes of a girl with Down syndrome. Arrow indicates the extra #21 chromosome.

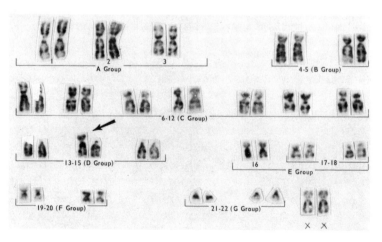

Figure 8. Karyotype of a girl with translocation Down syndrome. Arrow indicates the extra #21 chromosome, which is "translocated" or attached to a #14 chromosome.

It is important to find out whether or not a child has translocation Down syndrome, since in approximately one-third of these children one of the parents is a "carrier." Although this parent will be physically and mentally perfectly normal and will have the normal amount of genetic material, two of the chromosomes in this individual are attached to each other as seen in Figure 9, so that the total number of chromosomes will be 45 instead of 46. Such a person is called a balanced carrier or translocation carrier. Although the joint chromosomes in the translocation carrier do not alter the normal functions of genes or cause any abnormalities, there is an increased risk that the carrier will have more children with Down syndrome. Parents will then need specific genetic counseling.

The third, and least common, type of chromosome problem in children with Down syndrome is called mosaicism. Mosaicism usually occurs in about 1% of children with this disorder. Mosaicism is thought to be due to an error in one of the first few cell divisions (see Figure 10). Later, when the baby is born, one usually finds some cells

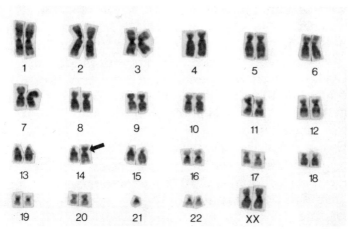

Figure 9.   Karyotype of a translocation "carrier." Arrow shows that one of the two #21 chromosomes is here attached to a #14 chromosome.

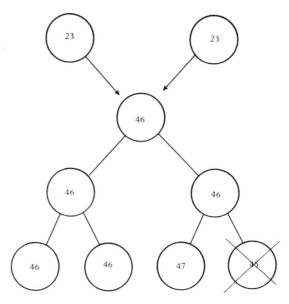

Figure 10. In mosaicism the "accident of nature" (nondisjunction) is thought to occur during one of the early cell divisions. Infants with this condition have some cells with 46 chromosomes and others with 47 chromosomes. Cells with 45 or less chromosomes usually do not survive.

with 47 chromosomes and other cells with the normal number of 46 chromosomes. This presents a kind of mosaic picture, hence the term *mosaicism*. Several authors have reported that some children with mosaicism Down syndrome have less pronounced features of Down syndrome and that their intellectual performance is better on average than that of children with trisomy 21.

Regardless of the type, whether trisomy 21, translocation, or mosaicism, it is always the #21 chromosome that is responsible for the specific physical features and limited intellectual functioning observed in the vast majority of children with Down syndrome. Yet, it is not known in what way the genes of this extra chromosome interfere with the unborn child's development leading to the physical characteristics and the deleterious effect on brain function.

In recent years we have learned that it is not the entire extra 21 chromosome, but only a small segment of the long arm of this chromosome, as shown in Figure 11, that is responsible for the problems we observe in children with Down syndrome. Many genes located on this part of the chromosome #21 have already been identified. Currently, numerous investigators are involved in studying the genes on this segment of the #21 chromosome to try to discover the mechanisms involved in its "malfunctioning."

During the past 30 years additional theories about the causation of Down syndrome have been proposed. Researchers have reported that X-ray exposure, administration of certain drugs, hormonal or immunological problems, spermatocites, and specific viral infections may cause Down syndrome. Whereas it is theoretically possible that these circumstances could lead to chromosome abnormalities, there is no definite evidence that any of these situations has ever been directly responsible for a child having Down syndrome.

One factor, however, that has been well known for some time is that the occurrence of Down syndrome is as-

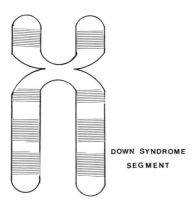

DOWN SYNDROME
SEGMENT

Figure 11.   Sketch of a #21 chromosome. The lower part of the long arm is called the "Down syndrome" segment.

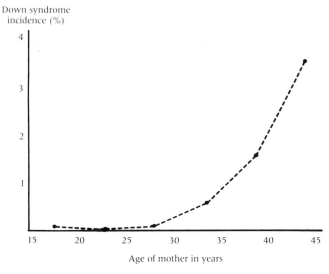

Figure 12. Relationship between maternal age and incidence of Down syndrome. As depicted, the older the mother, the greater the risk of giving birth to a child with Down syndrome.

sociated with the advanced age of the mother (that is, the older the mother, the greater the risk of having a child with Down syndrome—see Figure 12). Therefore, physicians and genetic counselors usually recommend that mothers over the age of 35 undergo a prenatal test to determine whether the fetus is affected (see Chapter 6 on "Prenatal Diagnosis").

Other investigations that have attempted to explain the faulty cell division leading to Down syndrome have not uncovered much new information in this regard. At present, we just do not know what makes cells divide incorrectly and why chromosomes do not separate properly. It is hoped that future investigations will shed light on these unknown factors.

Prenatal Diagnosis

Siegfried M. Pueschel

Although prenatal genetic counseling has been available sporadically since the early part of this century, new techniques developed during the past few decades, including amniocentesis, chorionic villus sampling (CVS), ultrasound examinations, and others, have revolutionized prenatal diagnosis of genetic and chromosome disorders. Since the introduction of these procedures (described later in this chapter), physicians and genetic counselors have been able to provide more accurate information to many prospective parents regarding the outcome of the pregnancy. Instead of discussing general probabilities of risk, the genetic counselor now often can tell parents whether the fetus does or does not have a specific genetic disease or chromosome disorder such as Down syndrome.

INDICATIONS FOR PRENATAL DIAGNOSIS

Since various techniques used in prenatal diagnosis have an associated risk to both mother and fetus, there must be specific indications for using these procedures. Currently, several factors are associated with an increased risk for having a child with Down syndrome:

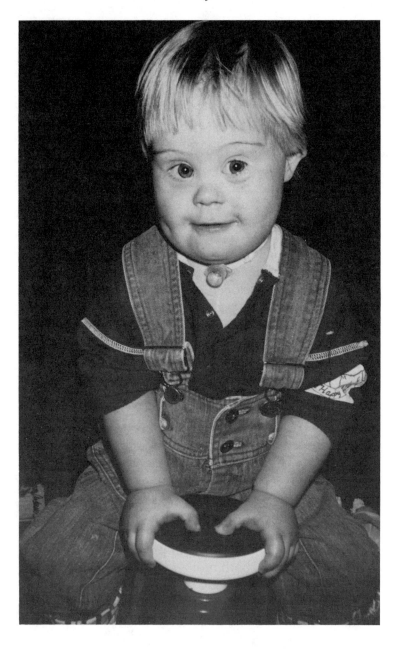

1. *Maternal age of 35 years or older.* As discussed in the previous chapter, it is well known that the incidence of chromosome abnormalities increases with advanced maternal age. The risk of having an offspring with a chromosome abnormality doubles approximately every 2½ years after the woman is 35 years of age. At the maternal age of 35 years, the risk that a pregnant woman is carrying a fetus with a chromosome abnormality is approximately 1 in 200 to 300 live births. At this age or older, the estimated risk of having an affected fetus is thought to be greater than the risks associated with amniocentesis. The risk of chorionic villus sampling is somewhat higher than that observed after amniocentesis. However, at the age of 34 or below, the risk of having an affected fetus is less than that of miscarrying as a result of these procedures.

2. *Paternal age of 45 to 50 years or older.* Although a paternal age effect also has been identified, this is much smaller than the maternal age effect. If the father is 45 to 50 years or older, there is probably a slightly higher risk of having an offspring with Down syndrome than in fathers below this age level. Some physicians recommend prenatal screening in this situation.

3. *Previous birth of a child with Down syndrome or other chromosome abnormality.* Many studies have shown that if a couple has a child with Down syndrome, the risk of recurrence is about 1%. Because of the increased risk, most geneticists and genetic counselors recommend prenatal diagnosis in families having a child with Down syndrome.

4. *Balanced chromosome translocation in a parent.* If one of the parents has a balanced chromosome translocation, for example if a #21 chromosome is attached to a #14 chromosome (see Figure 9, Chapter 5), there is a 50% chance that this parent may pass on this 14/21 chro-

mosome to an offspring. Therefore the parent has an increased risk of having more than one child with Down syndrome. This increased risk depends on the type of translocation, what chromosomes are involved, and whether the father or mother is the carrier. In general, the risk ranges between 2% and 100% for producing a child with Down syndrome. For instance, if a parent has a 21/21 translocation, there is a 100% chance of producing a child with Down syndrome. However, if a mother is carrying a 14/21 translocation, there is an 8% to 10% chance of having another child with Down syndrome in a future pregnancy. If the father is the carrier of such a chromosome translocation, the risk is slightly less.

5. *Parents with a chromosome disorder.* Although most individuals with a significant chromosome abnormality probably will not have children, some persons with chromosome disorders may be able to reproduce. For example, if one of the parents has a low percentage mosaicism for Down syndrome (that is, only a small percentage of the cells have the extra #21 chromosomes and the person may be otherwise normal), he or she is at a higher risk of having a child with Down syndrome than a person who does not have low-percentage mosaicism.

If a person with Down syndrome is able to reproduce, there is a 50% chance in each pregnancy that a child with Down syndrome will be born. There are about 30 reports in the literature indicating that women with Down syndrome have had children, whereas only one report has mentioned that a male with Down syndrome fathered a child.

In addition, there are other indications for prenatal diagnosis, such as a previous child with multiple congenital anomalies or spina bifida, or parents who are carriers of specific genetic defects. These and other indications, however, are not discussed here since they are not pertinent to Down syndrome.

TECHNIQUES FOR PRENATAL DIAGNOSIS

Techniques available for prenatal diagnosis of Down syndrome include amniocentesis, chorionic villus sampling, ultrasonography, and alpha-fetoprotein screening. Other prenatal diagnostic procedures such as fetoscopy, amniography, and X-ray examinations are not discussed here, since they are not used in prenatal diagnosis of Down syndrome.

Amniocentesis

In the mid-1950s, three important technical developments occurred that made prenatal diagnosis feasible: first, scientists became more knowledgeable in culturing human cells; second, the technique of chromosome analysis was improved significantly; and third, a safe and practical method of sampling *amniotic fluid* (the fluid surrounding the fetus in the mother's womb) was developed. When amniocentesis came into wide use in the 1970s, many professionals felt that by utilizing this procedure most fetuses with chromosome disorders, including Down syndrome, could be diagnosed. The procedure may be briefly described as follows.

Amniocentesis is generally performed at 14 to 16 weeks of pregnancy. Prior to performing amniocentesis, ultrasonography assists in identifying the location of the placenta and the amniotic cavity. In most instances a needle is inserted into the amniotic cavity under direct ultrasonographic guidance (Figure 1). Frequently, local anesthesia is applied before a needle is inserted through the abdominal wall into the womb and amniotic fluid is aspirated. This fluid is then centrifuged and the fetal cells that

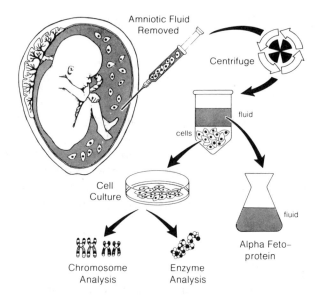

Amniotic Fluid
Removed

Centrifuge

fluid

cells

Cell
Culture

fiuid

Chromosome
Analysis

Enzyme
Analysis

Alpha Feto-
protein

Figure 6.1.   Amniocentesis. Approximately one ounce of amniotic fluid is re-moved at 14 to 17 weeks gestation. It is spun in a centrifuge to separate the fluid from the fetal cells. The fluid is used immediately to test for spina bifida. The cells are grown for 2 weeks, and then a chromosome or enzyme analysis can be per-formed. Results are usually available about 3 weeks later. (From Batshaw, M.L., & Perret, Y.M. [1986]. *Children with handicaps: A medical primer* [2nd ed.]. Balti-more: Paul H. Brookes Publishing Co. Copyright © 1986 by Paul H. Brookes Publishing Co.; reprinted with permission.)

are obtained are grown in culture and later used for chro-mosome analysis. Typically, it takes 2 to 4 weeks for suffi-cient cells to be grown for analysis, with results obtained immediately thereafter. During the 1970s several studies were done indicating that amniocentesis has inherent risks, such as miscarriage, injury to the fetus, or maternal infection. More recent studies, however, indicate that gen-erally it is a relatively safe procedure.

Chorionic Villus Sampling

Chorionic villus sampling became generally available in the United States in the early and mid-1980s. During chorionic villus sampling, a piece of placental tissue is obtained either vaginally or through the abdomen, usually in the 8th to 11th week of pregnancy (Figure 2). The advantages of this procedure over amniocentesis are that it can be done much earlier in pregnancy and that chromosome studies can be performed immediately, yielding much quicker test results. Studies so far have shown that the risks of this procedure are slightly but not significantly greater than that of amniocentesis.

Ultrasonography

In ultrasonography sound waves are sent into the womb, and as they bounce off certain structures such as an unborn baby, they are recorded on the screen of a monitor. Recent technological improvements in ultrasonography

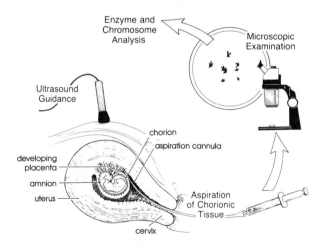

Figure 6.2. Chorionic villus biopsy. A hollow instrument is inserted through the vagina into the uterus, guided by ultrasound. A small amount of chorionic tissue is suctioned. The tissue is then examined under a microscope, and its chromosomes and enzymes are analyzed. (From Batshaw, M.L., & Perret, Y.M. [1986]. *Children with handicaps: A medical primer* [2nd ed.]. Baltimore: Paul H. Brookes Publishing Co. Copyright © 1986 by Paul H. Brookes Publishing Co.; reprinted with permission.)

have made it possible to identify certain fetal malformations such as heart defects during the latter half of the pregnancy. This method also has been used by some investigators to detect fetuses with Down syndrome by measuring the thickness of the skin at the neck area and the length of the leg bone.

Maternal Alpha-fetoprotein Screening

During the past decade prenatal maternal alpha-fetoprotein testing has become available. Initially, this test was used to screen for unborn babies with spina bifida, whose mothers usually have high alpha-fetoprotein levels in their blood during pregnancy. In the past 5 years, it has been observed that low maternal alpha-fetoprotein levels are often associated with chromosome disorders, in particular with Down syndrome. Several reports in the medical literature have described a high correlation between low maternal alpha-fetoprotein levels and the occurrence of trisomy 21 in the fetus. Therefore, today most obstetricians offer alpha-fetoprotein screening to pregnant women. Recent studies have shown that by using alpha-fetoprotein levels, the age of the mother, and specific female hormone levels, approximately 60% to 80% of fetuses with Down syndrome can be identified prenatally.

ETHICAL CONSIDERATIONS

There are only a few genetic disorders for which treatment can be provided to the fetus. For the majority of affected fetuses, such as an unborn baby with Down syndrome, no effective intrauterine therapy is available at present. Hence, some genetic counselors and physicians may recommend termination of the pregnancy if a fetus has been found to have trisomy 21. Although proponents of prenatal diagnosis and of termination of pregnancy if an affected fetus has been identified emphasize that each child should have the right to be born healthy, some professionals as well as parents of children with handicaps do not agree with the notion that every chromosomally defective fetus categorically should be aborted.

Of course, prenatal diagnosis has many potential beneficial uses, particularly in cases where therapy of the affected fetus is available or if parents can be counseled in regard to future reproductive risks. These justifiable uses, however, should not be overshadowed by allowing prenatal diagnostic techniques to become strictly an exercise in selective abortion. A parent of a child with Down syndrome expressed her views as follows:

> On the one hand we wanted and planned this child and didn't think we had the right to be choosy as to say we will keep it only if it's up to specs. . . . We never really know what we're getting when we elect to create another individual. And why assume that a child with a handicap will be a negative experience? For all the joy and richness they have brought into our lives, I am grateful to have all our children with all their weaknesses and strengths.

When Pearl S. Buck reflected on the meaning of her child with mental retardation she said:

> Could it have been possible for me to have had foreknowledge of her thwarted life, would I have wanted an abortion? With full knowledge of anguish and despair, the answer is no, I would not. Even with full knowledge I would have chosen life and this is for two reasons: first, I feel the power of choice over life or death at human's hands. I see no human being whom I could ever trust with such power. Human wisdom, human integrity are not great enough. Secondly, my child's life has not been meaningless. She has indeed brought comfort and practical help to many people who are parents of retarded children or who are themselves handicapped. True, she has done it through me, yet without her I would not have had the means of learning to accept the inevitable sorrow and how to make that acceptance useful to others.
>
> In this world, where cruelty prevails in so many aspects

of our lives, I would not add the weight of choice to kill rather than to let live. A retarded child, a handicapped person, brings his own gift to life, even to the life of normal human beings. This gift is comprehended in the lessons of patience, understanding, and mercy, lessons which we all need to relive and to practice with one another whatever we are.

The assumption that a child with Down syndrome or other chromosome disorder will have significant retardation or will never enjoy the delight of physical or intellectual achievement as "normal" persons do, is, according to some authors, not a valid reason to recommend pregnancy termination of an affected fetus. In general, an IQ score is a demeaning measure of human potential, and the assumption of mental retardation in a child with a chromosome abnormality such as Down syndrome is not a justification for aborting that fetus.

GENETIC COUNSELING

It is of utmost importance that parents be counseled appropriately when a fetus with trisomy 21 has been diagnosed. Several questions need to be addressed: What kind of information and in what way will it be conveyed to the parents? Is it possible for the counselor who has had only limited direct experience with youngsters with Down syndrome and who may know of the condition primarily from lectures and books, to give an unbiased picture of the life of the child with Down syndrome? How does a counselor best discuss with parents the various medical, intellectual, social, and other concerns related to caring for the child with Down syndrome? And in what ways do the counselor's personal attitudes, outlook on life, values, and ethical stance influence the parents' decision-making pro-

cess? These and other significant questions must be considered when counseling prospective parents.

Genetic counselors should provide factual information in an unbiased way to parents during the counseling process. If a fetus has been diagnosed as having Down syndrome, it is advisable that the prospective parents be introduced to a family who has a child with Down syndrome, so that they can gain a sense of what it means to have a child with Down syndrome in the family. The professional should never be the one who decides whether the parent should terminate or continue the pregnancy. This is a decision that only the parents can make.

An alternative to terminating the pregnancy if a fetus has been identified to have Down syndrome is to place the baby for adoption. Some parents who for whatever reason may be unable to rear and care for a child with Down syndrome and who may be appalled by the thought of aborting an affected fetus may want to choose this alternative. Thus, these parents would not have to deal with the trauma and guilt often associated with abortion. Since improved medical services and progressive educational opportunities have resulted in an enhanced quality of life for persons with Down syndrome, and since the majority of them have delightful personalities, these children are generally easy to place for adoption. Actually, there are long lists of families waiting to adopt children with Down syndrome.

Counseling should be noncoercive and respectful of parental views. It is paramount that counselors and other professionals realize that a child with Down syndrome is not necessarily a negative experience for a family and for society. Actually, persons with Down syndrome can have a real humanizing influence on society.

Physicians just starting their practice and other health professionals involved in genetic counseling should be taught the many ethical concerns relating to prenatal diagnosis. Service to humanity should rank high in their priorities. They should appreciate the dignity of human beings at any stage of life. They need to be aware that all human life is significant, and that a child's value is intrinsically rooted in his or her very humanity and uniqueness as a human being. Compassionate but objective genetic counseling should be solidly based on such values.

Physical Characteristics of the Child

Siegfried M. Pueschel

The appearance and functions of every living being are primarily determined by genes. Likewise, the physical characteristics of children with Down syndrome are shaped by influences from their genetic material. Since children inherit genes from both mother and father, they will, to some degree, resemble their parents in aspects such as body build, hair and eye color, and growth patterns (although the latter will be slower). Yet, because of additional genetic material on their extra chromosome #21, children with Down syndrome also have bodily characteristics that make them look different from their parents, siblings, or children without handicaps. Since this extra #21 chromosome is found in cells of every child with Down syndrome, it exerts its body-forming influence similarly in all such children. Therefore, children with Down syndrome have many physical features in common and look somewhat like each other.

Genes from the additional #21 chromosome are re-

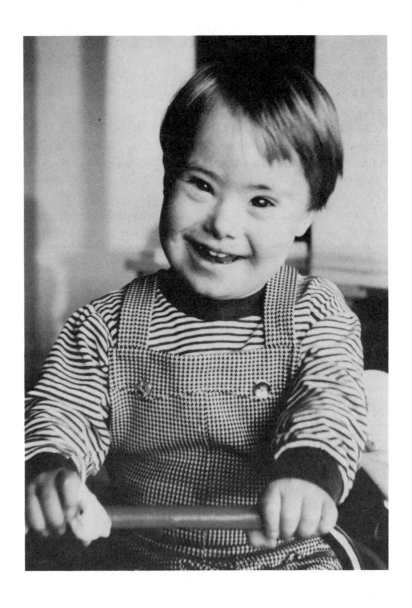

sponsible for the altered development of certain body parts during the very early stage of the unborn baby's (embryo's) life. However, we do not know how these changes come about or in what way genes from the extra chromosome interfere with normal developmental sequences. Moreover, we cannot explain why some children with Down syndrome have certain features or conditions, yet others with the extra chromosome do not. For example, we do not know why approximately 40% of children with Down syndrome have congenital heart defects, yet 60% are spared this problem. Much work remains to be done to answer these questions, work that, it is hoped, will help to illuminate the body's growth mechanisms in its early development.

The following paragraphs describe the physical characteristics of the child with Down syndrome. Although some of the characteristics occur with a high frequency and are considered typical of this syndrome, it should be emphasized that they usually are only minor findings and generally do not interfere with the child's functioning or render him or her unattractive. The physical features of the child with Down syndrome are important to the physician for diagnostic purposes. However, it should be emphasized that children with Down syndrome are more similar to the average child in the community than they are different.

The *head* of the child with Down syndrome is somewhat smaller when compared with normal children. The back of the head is slightly flattened (*brachycephaly*) in most of the children, which gives the head a round appearance. The soft spots (*fontanels*) are frequently larger and take longer to close. In the midline where the bones of the skull meet (suture line), there is often an additional soft spot (false fontanel). In some children there may be areas of missing hair (*alopecia areata*), or on rare occasion all hair may have fallen out (*alopecia totalis*).

The *face* of the young child with Down syndrome has a somewhat flat contour, primarily due to the underdeveloped facial bones and the small nose. Usually, the nasal bridge is somewhat depressed. In many children the nasal passages are narrow.

The *eyes* are usually normal in shape. The eyelids are narrow and slightly slanted. A skin fold (*epicanthal fold*) can be seen in many babies at the inside corners of the eyes. The periphery of the iris often has white speckles (*Brushfield spots*).

The *ears* are sometimes small, and the top rim of the ear (*helix*) is often folded over. The structure of the ear is occasionally slightly altered. The ear canals are narrow.

The *mouth* of the child with Down syndrome is small. Some children keep their mouth open, and the tongue may be slightly protruding. As the child with Down syndrome gets older, the tongue may become furrowed. The lips are often chapped during wintertime. The roof of the mouth (*palate*) is narrower than in the "normal" child. The eruption of the baby teeth is usually delayed. Sometimes one or more teeth are missing, and some teeth may be slightly different in shape. The jaws are small, which often leads to crowding of the permanent teeth. Dental decay is observed less often in most children with Down syndrome than in "normal" children.

The *neck* of the person with Down syndrome might appear somewhat broad and stocky. In the infant, loose skin folds are often noted at both sides of the back of the neck, which become less prominent or may disappear as the child grows.

On occasion the *chest* has a peculiar shape in that the child may have a depressed chest bone (*funnel chest*) or the chest bone might be sticking out (*pigeon chest*). In the child who has an enlarged heart due to congenital heart disease, the chest might appear fuller on the side of the heart.

As stated earlier, about 40% of children with Down syndrome have *heart* defects. Should your child have a congenital heart defect, you might hear your doctor say that he or she has a loud heart murmur. This may be due to blood rushing through a hole between the chambers, the result of a faulty functioning valve, or because of a narrow section of one of the large vessels. In contrast to loud murmurs heard in children with significant congenital heart defects, soft, short, and low-pitched heart murmurs are sometimes heard during the examination of children who have normal hearts. These minor or functional murmurs usually do not signify a heart problem.

The *lungs* of the child with Down syndrome are usually not abnormal. Only a few infants may have underdeveloped (hypoplastic) lungs. Some children, in particular those with congenital heart disease, may have increased blood pressure within the lung vessels, sometimes leading to pneumonia. With proper medical treatment, these infections can be controlled.

The *abdomen* of children with Down syndrome ordinarily does not show any abnormalities. The abdominal muscles of infants are sometimes weak and the abdomen might be slightly protuberant. The midline of the abdomen at times sticks out because of poor muscle development in this area. More than 90% of these children have a small rupture at the navel (umbilical hernia), which usually does not require surgery or cause any difficulties later. These hernias most often close spontaneously as the child grows. The inner organs such as liver, spleen, and kidneys are most often normal.

The *genitals* of boys and girls are unaffected in the majority of children. They might at times be somewhat small. Occasionally, the testicles may not be found in the scrotum during the first few years of life, but may be in the groin area or inside the abdomen.

The *extremities* are usually of normal shape. The hands and feet tend to be small and stubby in many children with Down syndrome. The fingers might be somewhat short, and the fifth finger is often curved slightly inward. In about 50% of children with Down syndrome, a single crease is observed across the palm on one or both hands. Fingerprints (*dermatoglyphics*) are also different from those of other children and have been used in the past to identify children with Down syndrome.

The *toes* of the child with Down syndrome are usually short. In the majority of children there is a wide space between the first and second toes, with a crease running between them on the sole of the foot. Many children with Down syndrome have flat feet because of the laxity of tendons. In some instances, an orthopaedist may advise that the child wear corrective shoes. In other children there will not be any need for special shoes. Because of the general laxity of ligaments, the child is "loose jointed." Ordinarily, this will not cause any problems, except when a joint comes out of place (*subluxation or dislocation*), as sometimes happens with the kneecap (*patella*) or hip. Often joint dislocation requires surgical correction. Many infants with Down syndrome have poor muscle tone, reduced muscle strength, and limited muscle coordination. However, muscle tone and muscle strength improve markedly as the child gets older.

The *skin* is usually fair and may have a mottled appearance during infancy and early childhood. During the cold season, the skin is often dry, and hands and face may chap more easily than in other children. In older children and adults with Down syndrome the skin may feel rough.

It should be reemphasized that not every child with Down syndrome exhibits all of the preceding characteris-

tics. In addition, some characteristics are more prominent in some children than in others. Thus, although children with Down syndrome can be recognized because of their similar physical appearance, not all such children look the same. Moreover, some of the features of the child with Down syndrome change over time.

As stated earlier, most of the physical findings mentioned here do not interfere with the development and health of the child. For example, the incurved little finger does not limit the function of the hand, nor will the slanting of the eyelids decrease a child's vision. Other defects, however, such as severe congenital heart defects or blockage of the bowel, are serious and require prompt medical attention. Many of the physical features described here may also be found in other children with handicaps and occasionally in "normal" children. Other rare congenital problems also occur in children with Down syndrome. They are not detailed here but have been documented extensively in the medical literature.

It is of utmost importance that the physician does not overemphasize the physical characteristics of the child, but rather presents the infant with Down syndrome as a human being who needs nurturance and love.

Medical Concerns

Siegfried M. Pueschel

In past decades most individuals with Down syndrome were usually not afforded adequate medical care. Often they were deprived of all but the most elementary medical services. Problems such as infections, congenital heart disease, glandular (endocrine) disorders, sensory impairments, and musculoskeletal difficulties were rarely treated appropriately. Early intervention, special education, and innovative recreational services were often nonexistent. Fortunately, the past few decades have seen major improvement in both the health care and provision of educational services for persons with Down syndrome.

Any exhaustive description of all of the possible medical concerns of persons with Down syndrome would be impossible within the boundaries of this chapter (discussions of these are readily accessible in the medical literature). Rather, I have chosen to describe the major medical problems encountered by individuals with Down syndrome, beginning with certain congenital anomalies noted in the newborn that require immediate attention. The discussion then moves to clinical conditions that occur often in individuals with Down syndrome during the subsequent childhood years, such as infectious diseases, increased nutritional intake, gum disease, seizure disorders, sleep apnea, visual and hearing impairments, and thyroid and skeletal problems. Lastly, the chapter examines some of the mental health issues observed during adolescence and in older persons with Down syndrome.

As stated in the previous chapter, persons with Down syndrome differ widely both in regard to the presence and degree of their medical concerns. Many organs within the body may be adversely affected, and persons with Down syndrome have more medical problems than those without this chromosome disorder. However, the majority of individuals with Down syndrome who are provided with appropriate medical and dental services will be in general good health.

CONGENITAL ANOMALIES IN THE NEWBORN

A number of congenital anomalies may be observed in newborn babies with Down syndrome, some of which may be life threatening and require immediate correction, whereas others may become apparent in the days and weeks subsequent to the child's birth.

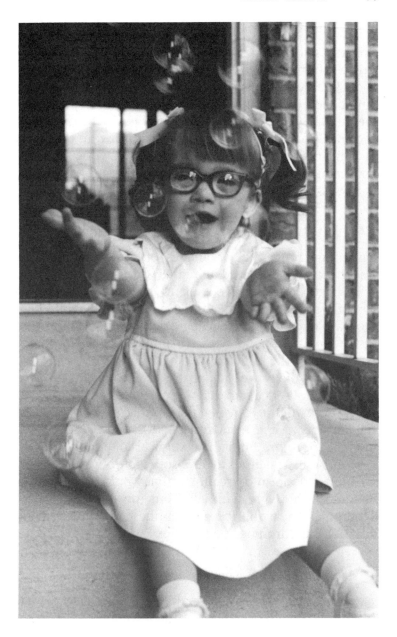

Congenital Cataracts

Congenital cataracts occur in about 3% of infants with Down syndrome. Because the cataractous changes do not allow light to reach the back of the eye (*retina*), it is important to identify children who have cataracts early in life. If the cataract is not extracted soon after birth, the child may become blind. The removal of the cataract from the eye is usually an easy operation in the hands of a good pediatric ophthalmologist. Subsequently, appropriate correction with glasses or contact lenses will ensure adequate vision.

Congenital Anomalies of the Gastrointestinal Tract

Numerous congenital anomalies of the gastrointestinal tract have been observed in infants with Down syndrome. It has been estimated that up to 12% of children with Down syndrome have such anomalies. There could be a blockage of the food pipe (*esophageal atresia*), a connection of the food pipe (*esophagus*) with the air pipe (*trachea*), a narrowing of the outlet of the stomach (*pyloric stenosis*), a blockage of the bowel adjacent to the stomach (*duodenal atresia*), an absence of certain nerves in some parts of the bowel (*Hirschsprung disease*), the absence of the anal opening (*imperforate anus*), and others. Most of these congenital anomalies require immediate surgical intervention to allow nutrients and fluids to be absorbed through the bowel. Of course, no form of treatment that would remedy these conditions should be withheld from any child with Down syndrome that would be given unhesitatingly to a child without this chromosome disorder.

Congenital Heart Disease

As noted previously in this book, congenital heart disease is observed in approximately 40% of children with Down syndrome. The most commonly seen problem concerns the central part of the heart, where holes in the walls between the chambers and abnormal development of the heart valves may be present. This condition is usually referred to as an *endocardial cushion defect* or *atrioventricular canal.* Other congenital anomalies of the heart may also be present, such as *ventricular septal defect, atrial septal defect, tetralogy of Fallot,* and others. It is important to detect heart problems in early infancy, because some children with severe congenital heart disease may develop heart failure, thrive poorly, and/or may acquire increased blood pressure in the vessels of the lungs. Therefore, the newborn infant with Down syndrome should have an *electrocardiogram,* a chest X ray, and, if indicated, an *echocardiogram* (sound waves are sent to the heart and the reflected echoes are recorded showing anatomical details of the heart) and a consultation by a pediatric cardiologist.

Appropriate medical management should include the administration of certain medications such as digitalis and diuretics, if needed. It is important that prompt surgical repair of the heart defect be carried out at an optimal time in the child's life. Such surgery will then significantly improve the child's quality of life.

PROBLEMS OF CHILDHOOD

Infections

Some reports from the literature indicate that children with Down syndrome have frequent respiratory infections in early childhood and that such infections are more often seen in children who also have congenital heart disease. In addition, ear infections are common in youngsters with Down syndrome. Some adolescents have recurrent skin infections, primarily at the thighs and buttocks.

Questions have been raised whether children with Down syndrome have appropriate protection and resistance against infections. Although no serious defects of the immune system occur in children with Down syndrome, a number of subtle changes exist in their bodies' defense mechanisms. Investigators have reported that the children often have fewer blood cells (specific lymphocytes), which are important in the general defense of the body. The function of some of these cells (B and T lymphocytes) also has been found to be abnormal in children with Down syndrome.

Nutritional Concerns

During early infancy feeding problems and poor weight gain may be observed in some children with Down syndrome, in particular in those with severe congenital heart disease. The children might feed poorly and fail to thrive. As soon as the congenital heart defect is repaired, however, children with Down syndrome start gaining weight adequately.

Increased weight gain is often noted in many adolescents and older persons with Down syndrome. This is probably due to decreased physical activity and increased food intake. However, some youngsters with Down syndrome have increased weight gain even with a normal caloric intake. It is important that from early childhood on, children with Down syndrome have a suitable diet to avoid excessive weight gain. Appropriate eating habits, a balanced diet, avoidance of high caloric foods, and regular physical exercise are paramount for all children, including those with Down syndrome.

Gum Disease

Although delay in tooth eruption, abnormalities of tooth shape, and sometimes congenital absence or fusion of teeth are observed in children with Down syndrome, the most devastating dental concern relates to gum problems (*periodontal disease* and *gingivitis*). Many reports in the literature describe an increased frequency of gum disease in individuals with this chromosome disorder. Therefore, it is important that persons with Down syndrome have regular dental examinations, that they practice appropriate dental hygiene, receive fluoride treatments, follow good dietary habits, and, if needed, undergo restorative care, which in turn should prevent dental caries and periodontal disease.

Seizure Disorders

There are various forms of seizures in children with Down syndrome. Some studies claim that up to 8% of individuals with Down syndrome have some form of seizure disorder. A particular form of seizure, called *infantile spasms*, is observed in children between 5 and 10 months of age. This seizure form is difficult to treat effectively in children who do not have Down syndrome. However, a specific treatment (*ACTH, adrenocorticotropic hormone*) is often effective in children with Down syndrome who have infantile spasms. After ACTH treatment, children usually display marked improvement in their development. Other forms of seizures (*grand mal, complex seizures*, and others) are seen in some children during childhood and adolescence. In particular, older persons with Down syndrome may develop seizures that may be associated with Alzheimer disease. It is essential to recognize specific forms of seizure disorders in persons with Down syndrome and to initiate prompt treatment with appropriate medications.

Sleep Apnea

In recent years, the medical literature has contained several reports of *sleep apnea* in individuals with Down syndrome. Sleep apnea is primarily due to some obstruction in the back of the throat by large tonsils and adenoids. Children with sleep apnea usually display noisy breathing, they snore, and have short episodes during sleep when they do not breathe. Sleep apnea may cause a reduced oxygen content in the blood and sleepiness and poor concentration during the day. A few children who exhibit this disorder in association with large tonsils and adenoids and/or obesity have developed increased blood pressure in the vessels of the lungs and subsequent heart failure. Children who have been diagnosed to have sleep apnea due to upper airway obstruction often can be treated successfully by surgical removal of the enlarged tonsils and adenoids.

Visual Impairments

Many children with Down syndrome have eye problems. It has been reported that up to 50% of children are nearsighted and that another 20% are farsighted. Some infants have been found to have blocked tear ducts. Numerous children are cross-eyed (*strabismus*), have inflammation of the eyelid margins (*blepharitis*), and sometimes rapid eye

movements (*nystagmus*). In addition to congenital cataracts, as already mentioned, many persons with Down syndrome may develop cataracts during their adult life. A disorder of the cornea (*keratoconus*) occurs in approximately 2% to 7% of individuals with Down syndrome.

Since children with Down syndrome often have eye disorders, they should be examined by a competent pediatric ophthalmologist regularly. Normal vision is important for any child. However, if a child has mental retardation, as do most youngsters with Down syndrome, an additional handicap of sensory impairment may further limit the child's overall functioning and may prevent him or her from participating in significant learning processes.

Hearing Deficits

Many children with Down syndrome (60% to 80%) have been found to have a mild to moderate hearing impairment. This may be due to increased wax (*cerumen*) in the ear canal, frequent ear infections, fluid accumulation in the middle ear, and/or abnormally shaped small bones (*ossicles*) in the middle ear that ordinarily transmit the sound from the eardrum to the inner ear. Sometimes there is a problem with drainage of fluid from the middle ear to the throat because of congestion, upper respiratory infections, large adenoids, or *Eustachian tube* (connection between middle ear and throat) dysfunction. Children should have routine hearing assessments, at least annually. If a hearing deficit is noted due to a middle ear problem, appropriate treatment should be initiated. This may include antibiotics, placement of ventilation tubes into the middle ear, and/or a hearing aid if the hearing impairment is moderate to severe. Hearing deficit due to inner ear or nerve problems (sensorineural hearing loss) occurs less often.

A hearing impairment in young children with Down syndrome may affect their psychological as well as emotional development. Therefore, proper assessment of the child's hearing and prompt treatment if a hearing loss is discovered are of paramount importance. It is well known that even a mild conductive hearing loss may lead to a reduced rate of language development in children with Down syndrome.

Thyroid Gland Dysfunction

Although most children with Down syndrome have normal thyroid function there is an increased frequency of thyroid problems in these children, when compared with "normal" children. The thyroid dysfunction could be due to an increased amount of thyroid hormone (*hyperthyroidism*) or a decreased thyroid hormone level (*hypothyroidism*). Hypothyroidism is much more common and has been found to be present in about 20% of persons with Down syndrome. In older persons thyroid problems may be observed even more often.

The thyroid gland has important functions within the human body. If an inadequate amount of thyroid hormone is available, the young child's intellectual development will be adversely affected. Therefore, it is important to examine regularly the child's thyroid function to prevent additional brain damage. If thyroid dysfunction is not recognized early, it may compromise the child's central nervous system function. Therefore, thyroid hormone treatment should be instituted if a person with Down syndrome is found to be hypothyroid. Optimal thyroid function then will allow learning processes to proceed.

Skeletal Abnormalities

Skeletal problems in Down syndrome are common and may be found in many parts of the body. The major concern relates to the easily stretched ligaments in these individuals (ligaments are made out of fibrous tissue that ordinarily holds the bones together). Thus the vast majority of children with Down syndrome have hyperextensible joints (sometimes referred to as loose or double jointedness). This may lead to an increased rate of *subluxations* (incomplete or partial dislocation) and dislocations of the kneecap and hip.

Skeletal problems in the neck area are observed more frequently in persons with Down syndrome. Large studies have indicated that the vast majority of children with Down syndrome (85%) have neither *atlantoaxial* (referring to the atlas and axis, the first and second cervical vertebrae) nor *atlantooccipital* (referring to the atlas and to the occipital bone of the cranium) instability. About 10% to

15% have atlantoaxial instability, and about 10% to 12% have atlantooccipital instability. Both conditions are due to the laxity of the ligaments in the neck area. Only a few children with Down syndrome (1% to 2%) have serious neck problems when the nerves of the spinal column are damaged owing to pressure from the neck bones (called *symptomatic atlantoaxial instability*). These children may have problems with walking, may complain of discomfort in the neck area, and may have specific neurologic signs. Surgery may be necessary to correct the problem. In the so-called *asymptomatic* form of *atlantoaxial instability*, X rays show a wide distance between the first two neck bones, without exerting pressure on the nerves of the spinal cord. In this case, follow-up is needed and special precautions should be taken. Individuals with atlantoaxial and atlantooccipital instability should not engage in certain sport activities that potentially could injure the neck. These individuals should be regularly examined by a physician knowledgeable in this area. If neurologic symptoms become apparent, surgical intervention may be indicated. Also, persons with Down syndrome who want to participate in athletic activities such as Special Olympics should be examined by a physician, should have a neurologic evaluation, and should have a neck X ray to determine whether or not they have a significant neck problem.

Both atlantoaxial and atlantooccipital instability in individuals with Down syndrome should be identified as early as possible because of their relatively high frequency and their potential for remediation. A delay in recognizing these conditions may result in irreversible spinal cord damage. All children with Down syndrome should have an X-ray of the neck (cervical spine) starting at the age of 2½ to 3 years. Because we do not know of the natural history of this disorder, repeat X-rays may be necessary.

ADOLESCENCE AND ADULTHOOD

Psychiatric Disorders

In recent years I have seen a number of individuals with Down syndrome who had psychiatric disorders such as depression, behavior disorders, and adjustment problems. Some young persons with Down syndrome have had grief reactions following bereavement. When an adolescent cannot cope following an identifiable stress, an adjustment disorder may develop. Although most disorders, particularly major depressions, have rarely been reported in persons with Down syndrome, recent observations indicate that they occur more frequently than was previously assumed. Once the diagnosis of a psychiatric disorder has been made, specific treatment and counseling should be forthcoming.

Alzheimer Disease

Another condition deserving special attention in the adult person with Down syndrome relates to the aging process. There have been many reports in the literature of an increased occurrence of Alzheimer disease in adults with Down syndrome. Although the brains of persons with Down syndrome 40 years and older have shown abnormalities usually observed in patients with Alzheimer disease, one cannot state categorically that the disease is present in all adults with Down syndrome. Many reports in the literature as well as my own observations indicate that many adults with Down syndrome are as "normal" as other handicapped people and hardly ever exhibit the personality changes or psychological problems observed in persons with Alzheimer disease. It has been estimated that about 15% to 25% of older persons with Down syndrome have early signs of Alzheimer disease.

CONCLUSION

Persons with Down syndrome may exhibit numerous medical problems, and at a higher frequency than in persons without this disorder. Yet many youngsters with Down syndrome do not have any of these conditions and are often in perfect health. It is important, nevertheless, for persons with Down syndrome to be examined regularly by their physician and dentist and to undergo certain diagnostic tests. For example, it is paramount that individuals with Down syndrome have hearing assessments, eye examinations, thyroid function tests, X-rays of the neck, and, if indicated, other important screening tests to identify potential health concerns early so that treatment can be initiated at once. If provided with optimal medical services to foster their well-being in all areas of human functioning, the quality of life of individuals with Down syndrome will be enhanced and their contribution to society will be substantial.

Treatment Approaches

Siegfried M. Pueschel

For almost a century, a multitude of treatments for individuals with Down syndrome have been reported in the literature. Numerous medications, including hormones, vitamins, sicca cells, dimethylsulfoxide, combinations thereof, and many other therapies have been employed in an attempt to improve the physical features and mental functioning of persons with Down syndrome. This chapter briefly describes these therapies as well as surgical treatments.

MEDICAL THERAPIES

Probably the first reported drug treatment was attempted at the end of the last century, when *thyroid hormone* was given to children with Down syndrome. Since then, many physicians have utilized and continue to prescribe thyroid hormone therapy in persons with Down syndrome. However, a controlled study in the 1960s in which a group of children receiving thyroid hormone was compared with a group receiving a placebo reported no significant difference in the overall function of the two groups.

Pituitary extract also has been employed to treat children with Down syndrome. Although claims have been made of marked improvement, the current consensus is that pituitary extract does not benefit these children's intellectual and social development.

Glutamic acid and its derivatives have been used for children with Down syndrome since the 1940s. Many workers initially reported positive results, but more recent studies have not supported those early conclusions.

Dimethyl sulfoxide also has been given to children with Down syndrome. In particular, Chilean investigators have claimed a marked improvement of intellectual functioning in children who had received this chemical. A short-term study in Oregon, however, did not reveal any significant positive changes in children with Down syndrome who were given dimethyl sulfoxide.

Sicca cell or dry cell treatment has been advocated in Europe for children with Down syndrome for several decades. Sicca cell therapy consists of injections of cells prepared from fetal animal organs, allegedly to stimulate the growth and function of the corresponding tissues in the human body. A recent West Coast publication has focused attention in North America on this form of treatment. Reports from the European scientific literature, as well as results from a Canadian study and a recent U.S. investigation, however, do not support the claims made by proponents of this therapy. Moreover, recent scientific publications suggest that animal tissue injected into human beings may produce a severe allergic reaction (anaphylactoid shock) and/or a "slow virus disease" many years later.

A variety of medications, including minerals, vitamins, enzymes, hormones, and other substances, referred to as the *U-series*, have been used by Henry Turkel to treat children with Down syndrome. Although improvements have been reported by Turkel and some Japanese physicians who used the U-series, a double-blind study carried out in 1964 did not uncover any significant difference in intellectual function between children given the U-series and others who had been administered a placebo.

A 1981 article claimed that three out of four children with Down syndrome had gains of 10 to 25 IQ points when given large amounts of 11 *vitamins* and 8 *minerals* over a 4- to 8-month period. Reduction of the physical characteristics of Down syndrome were also reported. Unfortunately, the study design was poor. There was no random assignment of children to study and control groups; there was unequal distribution between study and control groups; the study failed to control for seizures, unusual behaviors, or sensory impairments; three different psychological tests were used; and inappropriate test procedures were used to study thyroid function in these children. Subsequent studies that attempted to replicate this study using the same "treatment" approach did not find any beneficial effects.

Since it was reported in the mid 1960s that children with Down syndrome have low blood levels of *serotonin*, an important neurotransmitter, several investigators have administered the precursor of serotonin, *5-hydroxytryptophan* (a building block of protein) in the treatment of children with this syndrome. During a longitudinal double-blind study at Boston's Children's Hospital Medical Center using both 5-hydroxytryptophan and pyridoxine (vitamin B_6), it was found that these compounds did not have any significant positive effect on motor, social, language, and intellectual development of young children with Down syndrome. In spite of the negative results reported by several other investigators using these "medications," some physicians in this country and abroad are still treating children with Down syndrome with 5-hydroxytryptophan and pyridoxine.

In summary, I must say that no drug treatment to date has been found effective for children with Down syndrome. It should be mentioned, however, that recent advances in molecular biology make it feasible now to directly examine the genetic basis of Down syndrome. The challenge for the future is to further isolate, map, and characterize genes on chromosome #21 that are responsible for the physical characteristics and intellectual limitations observed in children with Down syndrome. Identifying the genes and their interference with normal development and counteracting the specific actions of those genes could provide rational approaches to medical therapy in the future.

CHANGING OR ALTERING APPEARANCE

Facial plastic surgery has been discussed in both the lay press and the medical literature during the past decade. In particular, in Germany, Israel, Australia, and only sporadically in Canada and in the United States, plastic surgeons have operated on persons with Down syndrome to improve their facial appearance.

Although the surgical procedures may vary according to the child's individual needs and the surgeon's preferred approach, surgery usually involves the removal of folds between nose and eyes, straightening out of the slightly slanted eyelids, implants of silicone or cartilage at the nasal bridge, cheeks, and chin, and removal of part of the tip of the tongue. Proponents of facial plastic surgery suggest that because the child's tongue is too large, surgery will enhance their speech and language abilities. In addition, it is claimed that after surgery, children with Down syndrome will be better accepted by society, there will be less drooling and less difficulty chewing and drinking fluids, and the children will have fewer infectious problems.

Although subjective observations made by some parents indicated that facial plastic surgery benefits people with Down syndrome, more recent studies have not shown any significant differences in the number of articulation errors found in the comparison of pre- and postoperative examinations in children who underwent tongue reduction surgery. Also, a survey of parental ratings on articulation of the surgery and nonsurgery groups revealed no significant differences between the groups.

Numerous issues concerning facial plastic surgery remain to be investigated and evaluated, such as: For whom is the facial surgery—the child, parents, or society? Will the child be involved in the decision as to whether surgery should be performed? What are the true indications for facial plastic surgery? How will the surgical trauma affect the child? Can one remove prejudice by improving the physical characteristics of the child with Down syndrome? What will the results of surgery mean to the child's identity and self-image? Should the degree of mental retardation be a criterion for who should and should not have facial plastic surgery? Other concerns relate to possibly inappropriate expectations for normality after surgery that may lead to denial of the child's underlying disorder.

At present, facial plastic surgery in Down syndrome is controversial. Instead of anecdotal reports, well-designed and well-controlled studies, with proper rationales and sound objectives, should be conducted. Whether or not facial plastic surgery will be beneficial to the children who are affected and will bring about better acceptance of people with Down syndrome in society can only be determined from the results of such investigations.

CONCLUSION

Although no effective drug treatments are available, people with Down syndrome should be afforded all of the medical and educational services offered to children without this disorder. Furthermore, their appearance, including hairstyle, dress, attire, and general hygiene, should be such as to enhance their acceptance and integration into society. People with Down syndrome must be accepted for what they are and accorded a status that both observes their rights and privileges as citizens and preserves their human dignity.

Developmental Expectations

An Overview

Claire D. Canning
and
Siegfried M. Pueschel

One of the most frequent observations made by parents of large families is that of the uniqueness of each child. Brothers and sisters may have a strong familial resemblance and may display similar behaviors, but each is a distinct human being with characteristics that are truly his or her own. These differences can make for a beautiful harmony, an interaction of strengths, joy, and humor that make life interesting and a constant challenge.

The diversity of biological factors, functions, and accomplishments that exist in all human beings is present also in children with Down syndrome. In fact, greater variation exists in nearly all aspects of their functioning than in the "normal" child. Their physical growth pattern ranges from the very short child to the child with above average height, from the very slim and frail child to the heavy and overweight one. Their physical features also vary considerably, as described in Chapter 7; some children display only a few of the physical features common in children with Down syndrome, whereas other children exhibit many or all of them. Moreover, the mental development and the intellectual abilities of these children span a wide range between severe mental retardation and near-normal intelligence. In addition, the behavior and emotional disposition of these children vary significantly; some children may be placid and inactive, whereas others are hyperactive. Most children with Down syndrome, however, display normal behaviors.

Hence, the past stereotyped portrayal of the severely mentally retarded, physically unattractive person with Down syndrome is certainly *not* a true description of children with Down syndrome as we know them. Unfortunately, until recently most articles and reports presented data predominantly obtained from institutionalized populations, with the result that parents were often provided with a poor prognosis.

Together, we parents and practitioners must work to dispel misleading reports of the past. At the same time, we

must champion early intervention, environmental enrichment, appropriate education, integration into and acceptance by society, and guidance to families, as vehicles for enhancing our children's lives. In the future, parents must be given more accurate and encouraging information. Indeed, the overriding purpose of this book is to convey to parents that there is hope, that the child with Down syndrome is, first, a human being with all of humanity's inherent strengths and weaknesses, and that there is a future for our children with Down syndrome.

This chapter discusses in more detail the observed biological diversity of children with Down syndrome and what can be expected regarding their growth, developmental accomplishments, and maturation. The information presented here is based on recent studies of children raised in the loving, accepting, and protective atmosphere of the home. We believe that such studies project a truer picture of their abilities.

GROWTH

It is generally known that the physical growth of the child with Down syndrome is slower. Our extensive studies support previous reports of reduced growth pattern. As in "normal" children, youngsters with Down syndrome span a considerable range in height. This variation in growth is determined by genetic, ethnic, and nutritional factors; by hormonal function; by the presence of additional congenital anomalies; by other health factors; and by certain environmental circumstances. It is to be expected that a child with Down syndrome who has tall parents will be taller than the average child with Down syndrome. Yet, the undernourished child, the thyroid hormone deficient patient, the child with reduced growth hormone, or the infant with severe heart disease will be expected to be smaller.

At times, parents ask whether there are medications that can accelerate growth. Although several hormones are known to influence longitudinal growth, we usually recommend specific hormonal therapy only if there is an indication for it. For example, if stunted growth is due to thyroid or growth hormone deficiency, then well-controlled hormone therapy should be instituted. Whatever the underlying cause of the growth deficiency may be, children should be treated appropriately.

In general, the expected height of the adult male with Down syndrome is approximately 4 feet, 8 inches to 5 feet, 5 inches, whereas the height of the adult female is somewhat less, between 4 feet, 5 inches and 5 feet, 3 inches.

WEIGHT

In addition to growth concerns, the weight of the child with Down syndrome often needs special attention. Since feeding problems are sometimes encountered during infancy, there may be reduced weight gain during early childhood. In particular, children with additional congenital anomalies, such as severe heart defects, gain weight slowly. During the 2nd and 3rd years of life, many children gradually start gaining weight, and from then on overweight may become a problem.

Some parents tend to be overprotective and offer the child an increased amount of food. However, once the child becomes accustomed to eating and snacking, particularly on foods with a high sugar or fat content, it will be difficult later to control this "habit." Some parents tend unconsciously to compensate the children with goodies, because they cannot, for example, run or perform as quickly as other children. Unfortunately, the more children snack, the less agile they are, owing to their extra weight. What one wants most is to make the child with Down syndrome as acceptable as possible to society. Therefore, it is important from early childhood on to encourage adherence to a proper diet. Good eating habits, a balanced diet, avoidance of high calorie foods, and regular physical activities can prevent the child from becoming overweight.

MOTOR DEVELOPMENT

Concerning developmental accomplishments, parents often ask when their child with Down syndrome will be able to sit or, finally, walk. Some answers to these and other questions relating to the child's motor development compared to that of the "normal" child are provided in Table 1. The data presented in the table are derived from the authors' own longitudinal studies as well as from recent reports on motor development in young children with Down syndrome. As mentioned previously, there is a wide

Table 1. Developmental milestones in children

	Children with Down syndrome		"Normal" children	
	Average (months)	Range (months)	Average (months)	Range (months)
Smiling	2	1½–3	1	½–3
Rolling over	6	2–12	5	2–10
Sitting	9	6–18	7	5–9
Crawling	11	7–21	8	6–11
Creeping	13	8–25	10	7–13
Standing	10	10–32	11	8–16
Walking	20	12–45	13	8–18
Talking, words	14	9–30	10	6–14
Talking, sentences	24	18–46	21	14–32

range of developmental accomplishments in children with Down syndrome. A variety of factors such as congenital heart defects or other interfering biological or environmental problems may cause a delay in motor development in some children. Subsequent chapters discuss in more detail the motor behavior of children with Down syndrome and approaches to enhancing their motor development.

SELF-HELP SKILLS

Similar observations have been recorded regarding acquisition of certain self-help skills in the child with Down syndrome for motor development. These are outlined in Table 2 along with comparable data for "normal" children. Of course, the child's readiness, his or her maturational level, and the approach to enhancing such skills are important factors that must be considered.

Table 2. Acquisition of self-help skills in children

| | Children with Down syndrome | | "Normal" children | |
	Average (months)	Range (months)	Average (months)	Range (months)
Eating				
Finger feeding	12	8–28	8	6–16
Using spoon/fork	20	12–40	13	8–20
Toilet training				
Bladder	48	20–95	32	18–60
Bowel	42	28–90	29	16–48
Dressing				
Undressing	40	29–72	32	22–42
Putting clothes on	58	38–98	47	34–58

MENTAL DEVELOPMENT

As in other areas of development, the intellectual abilities of the child with Down syndrome have always been underestimated in the past. Recent reports, as well as the au-

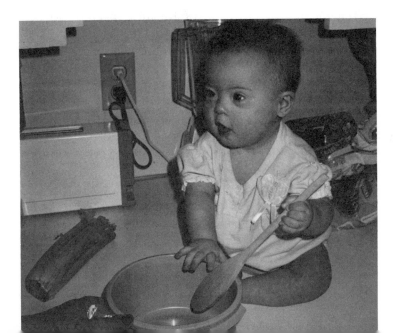

thors' own investigations, negate previous data indicating that children with Down syndrome usually have severe or profound mental retardation. Contemporary studies have found that the majority of children with Down syndrome function in the mild to moderate ranges of mental retardation, as shown by the vertical bars in Figure 1. Some children function intellectually in the borderline or low-average range, and only a few children have severe mental retardation. Thus, there is a wide range of cognitive function in children with Down syndrome.

Another misconception is that of the alleged gradual decline of mental ability in children with Down syndrome with advancing age. This has not been observed in a group of children with Down syndrome whom we have studied for several years. On the basis of this new information, the future for the person with Down syndrome should certainly be more optimistic today than ever before.

LONGEVITY

No reliable data are available on the life expectancy of persons with Down syndrome. Previous reports on this subject are outdated and no longer valid, given the dramatic increase overall in life expectancy. Today children are treated more effectively for respiratory ailments, heart defects, and other medical problems. Of greatest significance is that our children do not grow up in institutions, but thrive in accepting and loving home environments. The authors assume that the life expectancy of the individual with Down syndrome may be somewhat reduced but not to the degree previously reported. Some reports from the literature have mentioned that individuals with Down syndrome display an accelerated aging process, yet one cannot predict in early life which child will be so affected later.

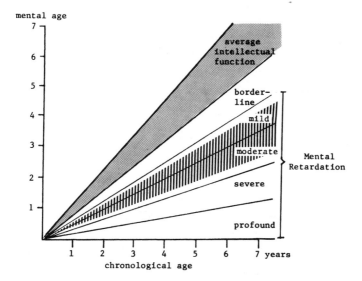

Figure 1. Top shaded area represents children with average intellectual abilities. When children function below "borderline," they are said to have mental retardation. The majority of children with Down syndrome function in the mild to moderate ranges of mental retardation, as indicated by the vertical bars.

Although children with Down syndrome show delay in all areas of biological functions, they do make steady progress in their overall development. We know that they possess definite strengths and talents that are a joy to perceive. Their sensitivity, their awareness of the feelings of others, their overall social development, and their sense of humor can bring so much happiness and satisfaction to their families and friends. True, there may be periods of apparent developmental standstill in some children; however, in the presence of loving home environments and the educational and social opportunities now available to our children, we usually observe significant developmental progress that would have astounded both parents and professionals in past decades.

Although comparison of various developmental parameters and the administration of tests are invaluable to

research in Down syndrome, it is important to keep in mind the intrinsic value of life, which transcends intelligence quotients and other developmental measures. It is, moreover, the knowledge that human beings of whatever physical or mental characteristics speak a common language that responds to affection, optimism, and acceptance. Coupled with the support of loving families and the work of professionals who create innovative programs and conduct research in biomedical and psychoeducational areas, the future has never been brighter for the child with Down syndrome.

Early Developmental Stimulation

Elizabeth Zausmer

Children usually are born with all that is necessary for contentment, at least during the first stage of life. Newborns typically sleep soundly, particularly after a satisfying meal. Their waking hours are enriched by sound and visual stimuli, while being held close, rocked, and fed. Much energy is also spent moving their arms, legs, and trunk, activities that are not only pleasing to the infants themselves but also bring about increased attention from parents or other caregivers. "Normal," healthy children display a sense of well-being and joy by cooing, kicking, and laughing. Their parents, in turn, respond with expressions of love, interest, and a variety of stimulating experiences.

Parents of children with a physical or mental handicap may at first find it more difficult to respond spontaneously in a similar way. They may need help to understand the child's slower progress in a number of motor and social responses. For example, a mother may interpret the infant's inability to suck as a rejection of her, rather than attribute it to weakness of the muscles needed to suck or swallow. Similarly, she may not know that the somewhat less vigorous movements of trunk, leg, and arm muscles can most likely be explained by muscle weakness and reduced muscle tone. We must remember that the child with muscle weakness has to work hard to achieve a result made with little effort by the "normal" child. In addition, sensory stimuli, such as voice, touch, and color have to be more intense to make an appropriate impact on the infant with Down syndrome.

EARLY INTERVENTION

The voluminous literature on early intervention with children with handicaps and my own extensive personal experience indicate that physical and intellectual limitations of the child with Down syndrome can be modified by competent management and early training. Feuerstein has stated in numerous publications that intelligence, as measured by traditional tests, is not an immutable quality but that it can be improved by intervention and mediation, in which the adult intervenes between the child and the environment. Most "poor performers" (Feuerstein prefers this term to "mentally retarded") have better potential for learning than their record would indicate. The child with Down syndrome is no exception. Direct exposure to stimuli and to life experiences, although needed by all children, are most frequently not sufficient to significantly change the learning patterns of children with Down syndrome. What is required, therefore, is a mediated learning situation, in which a parent or caregiver selects appropriate stimuli and discards inappropriate ones. Specific strategies are then used to augment the child's interest, attention, and skill level. Such intervention techniques can be learned and successfully used by parents of children with Down syndrome. Selected applications of such principles of mediation are included in this and the three following chapters.

Specifically, early intervention can focus on improving an infant's sensorimotor and social development. It also influences more complex learning processes. In recent years, psychologists and educators have generally agreed that it is the quality rather than the sum total of stimulation that shapes the physical and mental development of the young child. Therefore, the structure and content of an early stimulation program should be emphasized, rather than the indiscriminate use of nonspecific stimuli. This is particularly important in planning a stimulation program for the very young child with Down syndrome. Although it is true that this group of children shares many specific developmental handicaps, it is also true that wide differences are found with regard to their specific capabilities and shortcomings.

The motor development of normal children follows a fairly typical sequence: first lifting the head from prone, followed by rolling over, sitting, creeping, standing, and walking. Later we observe more complex activities such as running, climbing stairs, jumping, and skipping. Manipulatory skills also emerge in given sequences, such as holding, squeezing, reaching, pulling, pushing, and catching. Such skills, together with others in the social and cognitive areas, are gradually turned into activities that allow the child to explore the environment in more depth and detail. Although the sequence of motor developmental stages is fairly fixed, the use of efficiently mediated learning and practice situations contributes to the acceleration and quality of motor learning.

If the learning of such activities in the "normal" child requires a good deal of practice and experience, how much more work, patience, and training are needed for the child with Down syndrome! The latter has to overcome a number of hurdles that slow down the pace of his or her acquisition of motor skills. For instance, muscle weakness and poor muscle tone (*hypotonia*) make it more difficult for the child with Down syndrome to use the limbs and trunk, particularly when tasks involve the lifting of body weight against gravity (jumping, hopping, and climbing), lifting a load, or working against resistance (pushing an object or pedaling a bicycle). In addition, increased range of motion in joints (*hyperflexibility*) is often the cause of instability of joints, particularly the knee and ankle joints. Thus, the child with Down syndrome may be likened to an adult with weak or lax ligaments who does not have the stability to jump well or to hop on one foot.

Due to slower processing of information, it may take longer to elicit signs of curiosity and initiative in a child with Down syndrome. However, with adequate help, learning does occur, although at a slower rate. Indeed, the learning process is continuous, starting at birth with the experience of sucking, touching, turning, and lifting the head, combined with looking and listening. Although, at first, such activities occur reflexively, they are thought to result in pleasurable sensations that the child repeats successfully. For example, bright lights and colorful, moving objects entice an infant to turn the head to look. Later, in search of new and more interesting stimuli, the child explores a variety of voices, colors, textures, and shapes. Thus, the infant soon finds out that active effort leads to various rewards.

The infant with Down syndrome is frequently delayed in initiating motor skills such as kicking, wiggling, and rolling over. These activities lead to effective early exploration of the environment and in turn to continued learning. Parents should actively become engaged in helping their child with Down syndrome in these early learning experiences. Children who are not exposed to such gratifying experiences may become frustrated and express their frustrations by crying, refusing food, or by limiting their attempts to communicate. To avoid this, parents can help their child find satisfactory and enjoyable activities.

Whatever the level of achievement at a given time, there are always some sensory, motor, or simple cognitive tasks that can provide stimulation, experiences, and fun. It takes time and knowledge to choose wisely the components of such a program. The importance of engaging regularly and continuously in some form of basic skills is frequently underrated because results are not always readily visible. Perhaps it is easier to understand how physical skills are acquired if we remember how long it took us to perfect such skills as swimming, skiing, bowling, or chopping wood. These are skills that are based on previously acquired patterns of movement that were gradually combined into an organized, complex, sequential series of movements. With improved performance, the learner acquires increased feelings of pleasure, satisfaction, and success. The greater the ease with which a task is performed, the greater the efficiency. It is important for the child with Down syndrome to experience in early life as many pleasurable and efficient movement patterns as possible. These are essential for the development of more complex skills in the future.

STAGES IN SENSORIMOTOR AND SOCIAL DEVELOPMENT

The remainder of this chapter examines various stages in the development of a child with Down syndrome and analyzes some of the factors involved in providing sensorimotor and other learning experiences to help a child attain higher levels of performance and competence.

Positioning and Carrying

The very young infant with Down syndrome is apt to lie in a somewhat atypical position, the legs frequently spread apart and rolled outward, with the knees bent. This position, if it becomes habitual, can lead to faulty movement patterns in sitting and walking. While holding or carrying the child, his or her legs should thus be touching each other (adducted). Children with Down syndrome who have significant hypotonia are described as "floppy."

The position in which a child with Down syndrome is best carried varies with the individual, depending on the degree of muscle weakness in different body segments as well as on the overall developmental level. Generally, the young infant with Down syndrome needs slightly more support of the head and trunk than does the normal child. Although the head and trunk most likely have to be cradled at first to prevent sagging and wobbling, it is generally not necessary to restrict movements of the arms and legs by bundling these limbs while the infant is lying down, being fed, or carried.

Besides carrying your child in your arms, you may enjoy using a baby carrier in front of you or strapped to your back (papoose style) whenever your child is ready. You may want to change the infant's position from time to time by turning the carrier around, since looking out at the world is more exciting than facing the parent's back.

Tactile Stimulation

At a very early age, the infant responds most to being touched. Touch is a valuable source of information for the infant. Visual and auditory stimulation should preferably be combined with tactile experiences. Probably the most important early sensory experiences for the infant are those of being handled, held in the parent's arms, changed,

bathed, fed, and carried around. During these natural and spontaneous contacts with the body of a parent or caregiver, the infant obtains a good deal of sensory information. Such experiences may feel good or they may be unpleasant. Pleasant early experiences leave a favorable imprint and may contribute to the child's future physical and emotional well-being.

The following are some suggestions for tactile stimulation:

1. Place an infant on surfaces of varying textures, on rough as well as smooth blankets, and on different kinds of floor coverings or upholstered furniture. Whenever feasible, the infant's skin should be exposed to these various tactile stimuli.

2. Cover your infant's body with materials of different textures and weights, as well as with cool and warm garments. Since the infant's activity level may change under different conditions, you may want to loosen the garments to allow for freer activity, or use more restricting garments to elicit stronger movements against resistance.

3. Touch the child in a variety of ways, including stroking, rubbing, tapping, gentle tickling, and light squeezing.

4. Let the child touch you. Place the baby's hands on your face, hair, clothes, and on various parts of his own body. Encourage touching by placing the infant's hands on the bottle or on mother's breast during feeding time. Let the baby feel different shapes and textures of toys.

5. Children usually respond more actively when movements are accompanied by talking or singing to rhythmic tunes. Find as many ways as you can to combine motor activities with expressive communication.

6. When bathing an infant, do not restrict movements, but encourage splashing and other body movements while in the water. A pleasant and easy way to bring this about is to take your baby with you into the tub when you take a bath.

Oral Exploration

At this stage of development the infant can also be expected to explore by mouth all kinds of objects. Exploration by mouth is a very valuable experience that should be encouraged during early infancy. When the arms and hands are brought to the mouth, a movement pattern is practiced that serves as a model for most of the manual activities one engages in throughout life.

Oral exploration also encourages movement of the lips, tongue, and other structures of the mouth that are used later in chewing and swallowing as well as in speech. Therefore, "mouthing," at least in the first few months, should be seen as a valuable source of information for the child's perception of textures, shapes, temperatures, and tastes.

Visual Stimulation

Until a few years ago, it was generally believed that newborns and very young infants had a very limited capacity to focus on an object and had even less ability to differentiate between various visual stimuli. This viewpoint has been proven incorrect. It is now known that the infant is ready from the time of birth to look and learn. Therefore, your choice of learning situations that are offered to the infant is an important one. Infants like best to look at human faces. The distance from which an object is most effectively explored with attention and interest seems to be

about 8 to 12 inches from the infant's face. If a sound accompanies the visual presentation, the interest is often increased.

It is important to provide the infant with visual experiences that are attractive and meaningful. For instance, the feeding bottle might be shown to a child from various directions before being placed in the mouth. Similarly, the infant is encouraged to explore the rattle visually before it is brought near enough to be held. Or a parent's face can be moved before coming close enough to be touched. Colorful toys can also be effectively viewed and touched while the child is in a side lying position (pillow in back) or held upright.

Prior to starting to manipulate objects more purposefully, a child must be able to fixate visually, to organize, and to attend to an object. Children with visual handicaps are often considerably delayed in developing fine motor skills. They need special auditory and tactile training to make up for their visual deficit.

To evoke your child's attention and interest, attach colorful objects above the crib as well as on its sides. Commercially available mobiles can be used, but improvised ones serve the same purpose. Shiny spoons, colorful clothespins, fluttering multicolor tissue paper, or bells attached to a string can all be combined in various ways and attached to the bed. Leftover patterned materials cut into interesting shapes and sewn on colorful ribbons are preferable to unicolor materials. Brightly patterned curtains and sheets are also good visual stimuli.

It is furthermore important to realize that new sensations or impressions provide your child with a better learning instrument than do familiar ones. Thus, new stimuli should be brought into your child's life from time to time, rather than relying only on those that have already worked well. Whenever possible, take your child outdoors to provide experiences like looking at leaves, feeling a breeze, or listening to a variety of sounds. Such a visual stimulation program provides some basic skills in looking, focusing, and exploring, following an object through a wider visual range, and differentiating between various objects. These preparatory skills are needed for the later stages of active, purposeful grasping and reaching.

Auditory Stimulation

The word *communication* is used here to indicate a young child's capacity to express pleasure, comfort, hunger, pain, and other sensations and to respond in some way to what is being heard. Infants use facial expressions, grunts, babbles, squeals, cries, and other vocalizations as expressive communication. They show response to auditory stimuli by their facial expressions such as smiling, blinking, and grimacing, and through body movements such as kicking, squirming, or stiffening of the limbs. They react quite differently to a friendly, soothing voice than to one that is harsh or angry.

Infants also, at a very early developmental stage, differentiate a variety of rhythms, timing, pauses, and auditory levels of sound frequencies. Starting in infancy, several stimuli can be used simultaneously (e.g., singing while breastfeeding, touching while directing attention to a given object and at the same time talking about it, or dancing and singing to catchy rhythms and rhymes while holding the child in differing positions).

Generally, parents communicate spontaneously with their babies by producing sounds such as "baba, dada," and so forth. They also repeat vocalizations they hear from their child. Infants with Down syndrome, however, might produce sounds less frequently and with less variety of expression. The pitch of their voices has fewer highs and lows, and the expressive repertoire tends to be restricted. It seems to make good sense, therefore, to enrich the auditory environment by introducing a greater variety and intensity of vocal and other sounds.

The human voice attracts and holds the infant's attention better than any other auditory stimulus. One soon notices that particular sounds are preferred. If such sounds evoke pleasure and excitement, the infant will most likely kick his or her legs, move his or her arms, and wiggle his or her whole body. If the stimuli are very relaxing and soothing, one frequently observes more quiet movements of the limbs, some smiling, and an increase in focusing.

For the purpose of effective auditory stimulation, a wider variety of sound stimulation should be used:

1. Alternating between a low and a high-pitched voice, whispering, whistling, hissing, and blowing
2. Using words with a variety of vowels and consonants that produce expressive facial movements, since infants watch facial movements quite attentively
3. Frequent smiling, laughing, and giggling, since the infant reacts differently to each of these expressions
4. Using sounds and words produced with varying speed and rhythm, and sounds that come from different directions
5. Singing with varying modulations of voice

After a short period of auditory stimulation, there should be a period of observation to see how the child is reacting. If the response is a positive one, namely, the child seems to enjoy the experience and anticipates and participates during a repetition, the same type of stimulation should be repeated a few times. If the infant produces a new sound, the parent should imitate it and express pleasure by smiling, touching, or a simple verbal response. Then ample time should be given to initiate another output. Don't forget that your child derives just as much pleasure from hearing your response as vice versa. A combination of strong visual, auditory, and tactile stimulation (sensory integration) is optimally used to elicit effective responses.

The most important aspect of any stimulation program is to respond positively to reactions that show that the infant has been exposed to new learning experiences and has benefited by them. Even slow progress makes a difference in the child's capacity to cope better with the learning tasks ahead.

Gross Motor Developmental Stimulation

Elizabeth Zausmer

It is essential to start early to assist the child with Down syndrome to develop the interest and skills needed for a variety of physical and recreational activities such as playing ball, swimming, and moving to a rhythm. The joy and satisfaction that come from using one's body effectively will contribute toward making the child's future life experiences more rewarding. This chapter describes a number of activities that parents can engage in with their children to help stimulate their gross motor development at an early age.

HEAD CONTROL

Probably the most important goal in the initial phase of an early intervention program is attainment of good head control. Before an infant has achieved this stage of development, it is difficult to start working on more advanced developmental sequences. The infant finds it much easier to lift the head when lying on the stomach (prone) than when lying on the back. Normally, an infant can lift the head while lying on the stomach almost from the time of birth.

Children with Down syndrome frequently lift the head from prone position within the first few weeks of life. Sometimes a delay in head control becomes apparent when children are unable to keep the head raised for a longer period of time or when they fail to turn the head from side to side. If the child is placed prone with the head over the edge of the bed or a well padded table and a colorful toy is shown slightly above eye level, raising the head can be practiced successfully. The child then will follow the moving object by turning the lifted head from side to side.

When lying on his or her back, the child also needs extra stimulation to turn the head and to look at objects attached to the sides of the bed or strung across the crib. Except for a few smaller things that are fastened to a crib or playpen, the view from the crib should remain open and not be obstructed by padding on all sides, unless this is absolutely indicated for specific reasons. Your child should spend as little waking time as possible in the crib. Being in a playpen or preferably on the floor affords a better chance to learn through watching and listening. Once fairly good head control has been achieved, a child is usually ready to start pushing up and rolling over.

PUSHING UP

At about the time a child holds the head up and looks from side to side while lying on his or her stomach (prone) the first attempt at pushing up can usually be observed. The child may still keep the elbows bent and lean on the fore-

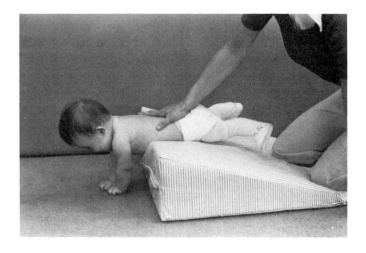

arms, but soon will start to lift the chest off the surface and arch the back. Children with Down syndrome need to strengthen the muscles in their shoulders, backs, and arms to do this. Even at this early stage of development, some variation of the push-up can be introduced to start developing strength in the muscle groups needed for creeping. Bolsters, blankets, or pillows shaped into a solid roll can be placed under the child's hips and stomach; yet the chest should not rest on the bolster. The hips are held firmly while the child is encouraged to lift his or her head and upper back. Interesting toys should be placed at an appropriate level in front of or slightly above the child's head. They can be moved from side to side to stimulate turning of the head and trunk. Instead of a bolster, a sloping board may be used on which the child lies face down with head and shoulders beyond the edge of the padded board. Excessive arching of the back should be avoided. You may also place your child with the stomach over your lap, with shoulders and upper back remaining free of support. Again, encourage lifting of the back and upper part of the trunk. Most likely, the child who pushes up on his arms with the elbows straight is ready to roll over. Some children, however, roll over before they push up.

ROLLING OVER

The motor developmental phase of rolling over is an important one for a child, because it expresses the wish and ability to move from one place to another and to explore one's surroundings. The child with Down syndrome may enter this developmental phase at a later age than the average child, and may also remain at this level of activity for a longer period before moving on to the next stages of crawling and creeping.

Parents should recognize that rolling over is a valuable experience and a good preparation for future, more mature motor achievements. Rolling over, if it does not occur spontaneously, should be encouraged. The child is placed on a mat, small rug, blanket, or folded sheet; two persons hold the mat at either end and gently roll the child back and forth by tilting the mat from one side to the other. Most infants enjoy this activity. It is a good steppingstone for a more active, voluntary form of rolling. It provides the experience of shifting the weight from one side to the other and also helps to overcome the child's fear of sudden movements and of changes in position.

When the child has become adjusted to being rolled, encourage more active rolling from back to side and side to side. A favorite toy is placed at a short distance, stimulating a child to turn his head toward the toy to look at it. The child will often reach for the toy and subsequently will start rolling over. You may need to help a little by moving the top leg across the other leg to initiate the movement. If your child enjoys being helped to roll over, a more spontaneous, active movement will follow.

Rolling from stomach to back is a more complicated

process, because more head control is needed as well as the ability to initiate the movement by pushing up on one arm. However, once your child has started to lift the shoulders and then turn the head while lying face down, it usually does not take long before active rolling in both directions is accomplished.

Rolling over should be encouraged. It is a good exercise for training body control and balance. It is also an early developmental activity that is brought about through a child's initiative, curiosity, and motivation to move and learn more about the environment.

SITTING

When a very young infant is pulled up to the sitting position, the head may wobble and drop backward. This is called head lag. The child with Down syndrome maintains a head-lag position considerably longer than the "normal" child. This is partly due to weakness of the neck muscles, but also because of the general developmental delay. Although the head lag decreases with maturation, it is important to encourage good head control in sitting as early as possible. Therefore, one should not let the child's back always rest against the mother's body or against the back of a chair while in the sitting position. Only minimal support should be given to prevent toppling over or sitting with poor posture.

If children are held firmly around the hips, they will frequently straighten their back to maintain good balance. It may be necessary to put one's hand around the chest of a child who still has poor balance in sitting. Such support frequently controls the wobbling of the head. Gradually, a child will learn to control the muscles of the neck and upper part of the back. The child will then sit with little or no support.

Even the very young infant enjoys being pulled up to a sitting position. When a finger is placed in the palm of the child's hand, the response is one of bending the arms. At a later stage the child will attempt to initiate the movement of getting into a sitting position. Encouraging a young child to grasp your finger, to bend the elbows, and to pull up to sitting, assists in the development of the muscles of the arms, shoulders, and trunk and also helps to improve head control. However, if there is considerable head lag, the head must be slightly supported to prevent it from dropping backward.

Most infants first sit in bed or on the floor by propping themselves up on their arms, which are placed at their sides or in front of them. Due to muscle weakness, this position is difficult to maintain for most children with Down syndrome. The arms may not be strong enough to carry the weight of the trunk, the back may be rounded, and the head may drop forward. Also, to maintain balance in the sitting position, the legs usually are spread wide apart.

Postures and positions that are detrimental to the development of good motor patterns should be avoided. Rather than permitting a child to sit for long periods on the floor, you should choose a sitting position where the legs are bent and held fairly close together and the trunk is held erect. An infant seat, small chair or any similar seating arrangement can be improvised in many ways. Sitting on a small chair leads to good postural patterns of head and trunk control. A chair must always be adjusted to the child's height and body proportions. A child's legs should not be spread apart too wide, and his or her feet should be placed in a good position on the floor. Such a sitting position gradually enables the child to shift some weight onto the legs and feet; this is a valuable preparation for future weight bearing in standing and walking.

If the child does not seem to be ready for unsupported

sitting, a strap or belt may be attached to the chair for stabilizing the hips. Such a strap should be attached to the chair like the seat belt in a car. Be sure to avoid placing the strap over the child's stomach or chest. A child who is tied to the back of a chair is apt either to slip down under the strap or slouch forward over it. A bouncer chair has to be elevated appropriately for each individual child. It might help to improve strength in some muscle groups if the child is able to sit with good posture and if his or her legs are used to push up. However, sitting passively slumped over in a bouncer chair serves no purpose.

With advancing age and maturation, more complex and demanding changes in sitting positions must be added to develop good balance. Balance reactions occur when the body is tilted forward, sideward, or backward, especially when such positions are changed fairly quickly. The following activities can be used to elicit balance reactions:

1. Lift and then lower your child while he or she is being held either in the upright or horizontal position, supporting the infant with your hands around the hips. If this does not seem to be a safe enough hold, place your hands around the child's chest.
2. Lie on the floor with your knees bent. Place your child against or on top of your knees and give support as needed. Rock your child forward, backward, and from side to side. Move your own knees off and back to the floor (this is also an excellent exercise for your own stomach muscles!).
3. While your child sits on your lap or knees, or on a bolster, tilt him or her gently forward, backward, and from side to side. Prevent excessive wobbling of the head, but don't give too much support to head and trunk. Remember that improvement in balance can only occur if the child makes a strong, active attempt at balancing.

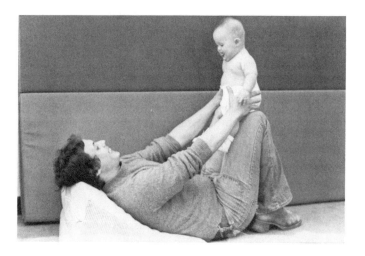

Sitting with the legs over the edge of a table or chair should be introduced as soon as it is safely possible. This sitting position allows for freer trunk movements, which, in turn, enables the child to reach in all directions to look at and reach for different objects. Besides the obvious goal of developing higher levels of balance control, the child gradually overcomes the fear of falling and learns to adjust to changes in spatial surroundings.

When an attractive toy is moved about by the adult in a well-structured situation, the child pursues the object visually, makes postural adjustments while reaching for it, and thus coordinates a number of body parts to grasp and manipulate the toy, perhaps handing it over or throwing it. Altogether, this is a sequence and combination of sensory, motor, cognitive, and social learning.

Gradually, the child is encouraged to shift more weight to the legs by leaning forward to reach for an object. This is similar to the first phase of standing up from a chair. It establishes a good pattern for the subsequent phases of standing and walking.

These activities or any others that serve the same purpose can be increased in complexity, intensity, duration, and speed to challenge the child to respond to full capacity.

GETTING FROM LYING TO SITTING

Most children need little practice in learning to move from a lying to a sitting position. They simply turn on their side, push up on their arms, and there they sit. In contrast, children with Down syndrome frequently follow a different

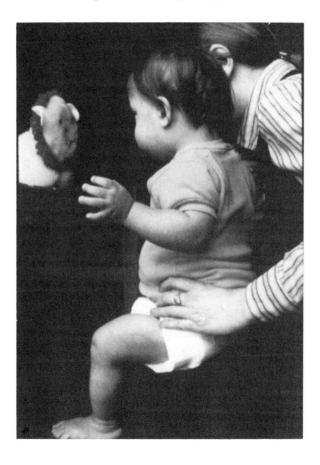

sequence of movements. They may roll over onto their stomach, then spread their legs far apart, and push up on their arms to raise their trunk off the floor. Although, at first, this may be the only possible way to come to a sitting position without help, it should be gradually discouraged. A more normal sequence can be practiced: the child first rolls to the side, then you should bend the hips and knees toward the chest. Next, place the child's hands on the floor near the chest. Then help the child to push up and to shift the trunk over the buttocks, thus coming to a sitting position. Gradually, you may want to decrease your assistance.

An extremely important milestone has now been reached, not only in gross motor development but in other respects as well. The youngster now can observe what is going on around him or her from a different perspective. He or she can reach for objects that were not accessible; can lie down and sit up, responding to different situations; can roll to a different place; and can then explore the new environment while sitting. Gravity has for the first time been conquered. Your child will be enchanted with this accomplishment and so will you!

The ability to sit up has opened new horizons for your child. The next stage of gross motor development, perhaps not easily achieved, is that of crawling and creeping.

CRAWLING AND CREEPING

The term *crawling* is used to describe the child who is moving about with his or her stomach touching the floor. When *creeping*, the child moves on his or her hands and knees with the stomach off the floor.

Almost all children crawl before they creep. The child with Down syndrome may lack sufficient muscle strength in his or her arms, shoulders, and trunk to come to the hand-knee position or to maintain such a position for any length of time. Therefore, getting to the crawling stage may be delayed. For many children it is easier to crawl backward or to pivot than to crawl forward. Some children prefer to hitch along on their buttocks.

Sometimes, a delayed start in crawling and creeping may prevent the child from successfully exploring the environment. Also, the child with Down syndrome may not exhibit the same degree of attention and initiative we observe in the nonhandicapped child. Therefore, one must find optimal stimuli that work best at a given time and in certain circumstances. Once this has been determined, such stimuli should be used until they can be replaced by new and novel experiences.

Most observations have shown that the color of a toy or other object influences the child's desire to handle it. Although children vary somewhat in their color preference, most prefer orange, red, and yellow to other colors. Whatever the color, an object that moves is most attractive to the young child. Almost all children show heightened attention or excitement when they look at an object that is pulled, swung, moved up and down, twirled, or spun around. Thus, mobiles, toys that bounce on springs, rings or bells attached to strings, and windup toys attract the child's attention most. Of course, always make sure that the toys or objects used by your child are safe.

The child who is well motivated to crawl or creep but lacks sufficient muscle strength may be helped by partially taking the weight off the limbs. Wrap a wide strap or a folded towel around the abdomen, then lift the abdomen slightly off the floor. Initiate the child's creeping movements by tapping lightly on the soles of the feet or by assisting the movements of arms and legs. Gradually, your child will participate more actively with less support.

This is the time to turn the creeping experience into

more meaningful structured and mediated learning. As the child creeps all around the house, the scene should be set to lead to discovery, exploration, taking options, and making decisions.

As an example, in full view of the child, drop a ball with a colorful ribbon attached to it into a box located on the floor at the other side of the room. The child usually will follow the parent's visual and auditory cues and prompts, will creep to the box, peek into the box, pull the ribbon that is within reach, and then try to pull the attached ball out of the box. Let us assume that the latter trial was not very successful. The parent then may tilt the box, thus making it easier to pull the ball out. Gradually, the box is returned to its upright position while the child learns to pull harder, with the arm or trunk being more elevated. A similar but more complex situation may then be set up: choose several differently colored ribbons, some can be attached to toys and others not, or the ribbons can be eliminated to encourage the child to make use of both hands to pull the ball out of the box.

Creeping upstairs is an excellent way to gain a sense of balance and to develop good movement patterns. Sometimes, a child who does not seem to want to creep on a flat surface will enjoy creeping upstairs with some help if a toy is placed where it can be seen and eventually reached. Although some children may not like to creep very much, you may find that if you yourself get into the all-fours position on the floor, your child will enjoy moving along with you. If you add a hide-and-seek game, it won't be long before your little one will come creeping around the corner looking for you.

At a more advanced stage of creeping, the action can be enlivened be setting the scene for creeping under tables, beneath chairs, or over boxes that have been turned upside down to create tunnels. To see a child creep happily all over the house is a wonderful sight. Now, the child has become your companion, following you around, eager to see and to be seen.

KNEELING AND KNEE-STANDING

After a child has mastered creeping, the time has come to pull up to standing. Most children come to the kneeling position and then use a chair, another piece of furniture, or the leg of a parent to pull themselves up to the erect position. The child with weak muscles may find it difficult to negotiate such a motor sequence, since its successful completion is dependent on muscle strength in legs, arms, and trunk. It is for this reason—namely, to strengthen muscles and to learn to maintain the trunk in the erect position— that training in kneeling is important.

A parent can help a child come to kneeling and maintain this position without fear or discomfort by holding the child's hips firmly and stabilizing the legs. You may want to place a toy on a chair or couch to motivate the child to stay in this position.

While kneeling, the child's shoulders, hips, and knees should be well aligned. The child who can kneel in this weight-bearing position has a better chance to develop a good standing and gait pattern. Coming up from kneeling to standing should now be practiced in the manner that any child would use spontaneously—namely, placing one leg in front and then gradually pulling up to a standing position. Generally, the preferred leg is used to push up while balance is maintained by holding on to a stable object such as a chair, sofa, or small table.

Kneeling is a good preparation for standing and walking because this position has a lower center of gravity as compared to full standing and also affords more stability for balance. In kneeling, the child can practice and become accustomed to shifting the weight from one leg to the other, which is a basic step in preparation for walking.

STANDING

Most children who have learned to pull themselves up proceed rather quickly to standing unsupported for longer periods of time. They rarely spend much time standing before they take off and start walking. By now their balance is fairly well established. When they have reached this maturational stage they can progress fairly quickly to unsupported walking. This is the reason why many parents cannot remember at what age their child started to stand, whereas they are apt to recall without difficulty how old their child was when he or she took his or her first step.

Children with Down syndrome may follow a somewhat different progression of motor development. They stand later than the "normal" child. Usually, they need support for a longer time period before they can stand by themselves. There are many reasons for this delay. Muscle weakness of the antigravity muscles of the legs and trunk often delay the attainment of the erect position. Also, children who have weak muscles are frequently more fearful of standing unsupported.

In preparation for correct weight bearing in standing and walking, some activities may be used that were suggested previously for the sitting position. A child with Down syndrome will most likely stand at first with the legs spread widely apart and the feet turned slightly outward. It can be expected that the inner arches are quite flat (pronated). This position affords better balance and stability. It is a position that, however, should be changed with time.

One of the first steps in encouraging proper standing is

to make sure that the child's body weight is distributed correctly and that it is properly shifted to the legs. The child must acquire the sensation of firmly standing with the weight on legs and feet, rather than shifting it onto a supporting object such as a chair or low table. One way to achieve proper weight bearing is to push down gently on the child's hips to elicit a reaction of resisting this downward push. This, in turn, will result in an attempt to straighten hips and knees and to keep the trunk erect. Gradually, the child will develop confidence in the ability to stand independently while support is decreased.

To overcome the fear of standing without support, it frequently helps to give the child a large ball to hold with both hands, to reach for and hold a suspended toy, to touch a parent's hair or face, or, generally, to engage in some movement that diverts attention from the threat of losing balance.

Standing on tiptoes should be encouraged. Several studies have pointed out that the calf muscles are frequently one of the weakest muscle groups in children with Down sydrome. Pushing the feet down against manual resistance during the prewalking stage is good preparation for later tiptoe standing and walking.

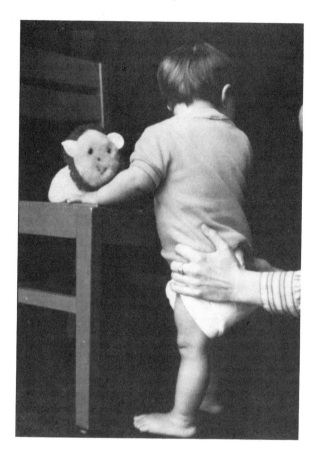

WALKING

Although standing and walking are often considered one entity, they are quite different phases of motor development. Although assuming an erect body position and maintenance of balance are needed for both activities, a third component is introduced in walking—namely, the ability to propel the body forward.

A child who spontaneously starts to walk has most likely acquired sufficient balance to stand on one leg while the other is swinging forward. The weight can then be shifted to what becomes the supporting leg. This is the reason that during the preceding training for correct standing, a great deal of time was spent learning to shift the weight from one leg to the other. For a child with Down syndrome, walking may present a considerable hurdle. Even after having mastered standing on both legs without support, standing on one leg appears more difficult. Therefore, the transition from supported to unsupported walking is frequently delayed.

The postural characteristics of children with Down syndrome that were seen in standing may still be present in walking. The legs are spread apart, the knees pointed outward and pushed slightly backward, and the feet are flat on the floor. The previously described measures to avoid or to minimize such faulty patterns might again have to be taken.

Most children cruise holding on to a sofa or a low table for a short time period before taking off on their own. It frequently takes the child with Down syndrome longer to achieve this motor act. The child also may continue to use this safe means of ambulation longer before venturing to take the first unsupported step.

Although it is alright for the parents to hold the child's hands during the first stage of walking when really needed, prolonged assistance is not the best way for the child to gain confidence, experience, and balance. The child should not be supported by the arms held above shoulder level in the so-called "high guard" position. A better way is to face the child, who walks with the body weight shifted forward to the parent's outstretched hand or to a chair or doll carriage, for example.

Studies published in the last few years have documented that the age at which children with Down syndrome start walking varies considerably (see also Chapter 10). Early intervention and early surgery for congenital heart disease have resulted in more advanced gross motor

development for these children. Other serious medical conditions, as well as frequent hospitalizations, may further delay the child's developmental milestones. One has to be careful not to use the age of walking as an indicator of how well a child with Down syndrome will do at later developmental stages. It should also be understood that gross motor development such as sitting, standing, and walking is frequently less delayed than is acquisition of language.

A careful, early assessment of the characteristics of gait is a most important feature of the child's motor developmental program. The evaluation is usually done by a physical therapist or specialist in early child development who plans the intervention program that will best fit the special needs of an individual child. Faulty motor patterns should be prevented before they become part of a child's repertoire that may be difficult to correct later on.

RUNNING

In running, the weight is shifted faster from one leg to the other than it is in walking. There is also a need to propel the body forward and to maintain balance during movements performed at greater speed. A certain degree of strength in the calf muscles as well as in other muscle groups is needed for the forward thrust of the body. Normally, the swinging of the arms makes running a smooth, rhythmic performance.

The child with muscle weakness frequently encounters some difficulties, both in maintaining the erect position and in propelling the body forward. The child may run slowly and awkwardly, barely lifting the feet off the floor while the arms are frequently held at or near shoulder level for better balance.

The following are a few of the activities that have been used successfully to prevent faulty motor patterns:

1. High stepping or stepping over hurdles such as boxes, boards, or a rope; lifting knees to the chest while running in place; and stepping up on high steps, stools, or low chairs
2. Walking on tiptoes and reaching for toys placed at a high level
3. Balancing on one leg, first with support, then gradually with less support; walking on a board placed on the floor or slightly raised off the floor.
4. Swinging arms in alternate, rhythmic movements; hitting a soft object such as a suspended ball with alternate arms; throwing a ball with alternate hands; beating a drum with two sticks; and marching while tapping on the lifted knee with the opposite hand.

For a child who does not spontaneously begin to walk, one must find a way to encourage the child's initiative and sense of competition. Whenever possible, enjoyable group activities should be used, since they often result in success. Squatting down and coming up from squatting are activities that strengthen the antigravity muscles of the trunk and legs. Most children enjoy picking up objects

from the floor or playing in the squatting position. The child with Down syndrome frequently prefers to sit down rather than squat, since the latter motor act is a more demanding position to maintain with insufficient muscle strength. Thus, whenever possible, squatting should be encouraged, as well as frequent changes from the sitting position to the standing position.

CLIMBING

Climbing stairs is another activity that assists in developing balance and that strengthens the leg muscles. A child with delayed motor development and weak musculature tends to hitch upstairs and slide downstairs on the buttocks rather than walk erect. Climbing stairs should be practiced early and frequently, first with two-hand support that is gradually decreased to one-hand support, until sufficient balance is present to manage stairs unsupported. Of course, at all times, the child should be protected from falling downstairs.

JUMPING AND HOPPING

Jumping and hopping are activities that demand a higher degree of balance and propulsion than is needed in running. Both are excellent motor activities for a child who needs to develop balance and muscle strength. First, under supervision, jumping up and down in place may be practiced on an old mattress or couch. As the child's skills improve, a soft rug should be used. Jumping alone is not much fun, but jumping with parents, brothers, sisters, or friends accompanied by a lively rhythm is enjoyable. Jumping and hopping can also be incorporated into all kinds of games such as imitating the movements of animals, jumping along lines drawn on the floor, jumping over obstacles, or jumping down from steps. These are only a few of the many motor skills that prepare a child to handle unexpected changes in body position and speed of movement.

Some children are not very interested in gross motor activities and sports and may prefer more sedentary activities. Other children may not participate because they have never experienced success and would rather not risk repeated failure. Failure produces an increasing sense of frustration, and the child will soon give up striving to perform better. In contrast, the satisfaction derived by having succeeded and having pleased a parent or teacher is a desirable reinforcement at an early age, when the child is not yet mature enough to derive satisfaction from a well-executed motor act. The reward can be a hug, the opportunity to watch a special television program, a visit with a

favorite friend, or a trip to a store. Food as the main form of reinforcement should be used sparingly, since it may become the preferred gratification, later often resulting in increased weight gain.

There is no reason to assume that persons with Down syndrome cannot achieve success in sports or other recreational pursuits. In fact, their body skills may later be their most valuable means of competition, as has been shown effectively by the Special Olympics. Even apart from competition, bowling, dancing, swimming, skiiing, and other similar activities can greatly enrich a peron's life.

13

Fine Motor Skills and Play

The Road to Cognitive Learning

Elizabeth Zausmer

A classic statement of Maria Montessori may introduce this chapter: "The hands are the instruments of man's intelligence."

The child with Down syndrome—like any other child—is ready to learn at the time of birth. An infant usually first acquires gross motor skills before becoming maturationally ready to engage in fine motor skills of any magnitude or complexity. Such sequential development does not necessarily apply to the child with Down syndrome, who may be delayed in gross motor development because of significant muscle weakness, congenital heart disease, or other physical defects. Such a child may be ready maturationally for more advanced fine motor skills before becoming competent in certain gross motor activities.

A thorough evaluation of the child's vision, attention span, and level of cognitive development is needed. Muscle strength and muscle control of a child's shoulder girdle and arms have to be checked before a home program, geared to the needs of the individual child, can be planned. Whatever the level of your child's ability, fine motor stimulation and play should combine a variety of learning experiences. A carefully structured learning situation should be provided from an early age.

FINE MOTOR STIMULATION AND BASIC MANIPULATION

At birth and during the first few weeks thereafter, the infant grasps an object placed in the hand. This is initially a "reflexive" grasp. Infants seem to prefer to grasp long and slender objects to short, round ones. Handles of spoons, clothespins, and similar objects attract their attention. When a child shows readiness for reaching, a toy or an ob-

ject should be placed in a position that requires a certain amount of effort to obtain it. The child eventually must be able to get hold of the toy rather than to give up in frustration. An observant parent will appreciate the child's efforts and will offer rewards.

The child who has muscle weakness and needs more stability to carry out motor activities has to be positioned more carefully to make maximal use of all available muscle strength in the arms, shoulder girdle, and trunk. You may want to refer to the previously outlined positions of lying on the side, on the stomach, or sitting in order to decide which one is best suited for a specific task. In addition, you can help your child by positioning toys in a way that allows the arms to be supported comfortably so they can be brought in front of the child. Such a position also provides a good angle of vision. Sometimes a child is left with toys placed too high on a table, making it difficult to reach. If toys are placed too low, poor postural and visual patterns result. Then the child may be sitting with the back very rounded, the head held too close to the play material, or the arms held in cramped positions and unable to move freely.

Young infants initially use raking movements to pick up an object. They take hold of it with the entire hand, which is called palmar grasp. Subsequently, a thumb-index finger grasp develops, making it possible to pick up and handle smaller objects. Children with Down syndrome start later than the average child in swinging the thumb around the palm of the hand. The thumb-index finger grasp, also referred to as pincer grasp, can be practiced by placing and holding your child's thumb and index finger around an appropriate object such as a small block, a paper ball, or a raisin. By applying light pressure over the child's hand to convey the feeling of holding the object and repeatedly using the word "hold," the meaning of the word is gradually established. Soon, your child can be encouraged to pick up small objects without help. A child who still prefers to use the palmar grasp will start to use the pincer grasp if an object is held out or handed to him or her, rather than placed on a table to be picked up. As your child's dexterity improves, his or her desire to pick up small objects such as pieces of crackers, cookies, cereal, or raisins can be used to encourage more frequent use of the pincer grasp.

Young children with Down syndrome need extra stimulation, encouragement, guidance, and mediation to become engaged in basic manipulatory skills. They have to be helped to explore objects manually as well as visually, and to apply such experiences to cognitive learning. Opportunities for such early learning experiences in infancy were discussed in Chapter 11. This section provides additional suggestions for a later stage of development.

At the table, let your child's hands explore various types of food to learn the difference between solids and liquids and warm and cold foods. Applesauce, warm cereal, cold ice cream, sticky marmalade, and peanut butter can be licked off fingers. Once the path from finger to mouth has been well established, finger feeding soon will follow.

Learning to use both hands simultaneously and to transfer an object from one hand to the other occurs spontaneously in the "normal" child. However, it needs to be practiced with the child who shows a developmental delay in fine motor skills. Playing Pat-a-Cake is a fun way to interest a child in using both hands simultaneously. Hold your child's hands in your own and clap them together while singing or listening to a tune. If the child starts to participate, reward him or her by smiling and hugging. As your child makes progress in these activities, you can decrease your assistance gradually.

Another activity may involve placing a large ball be-

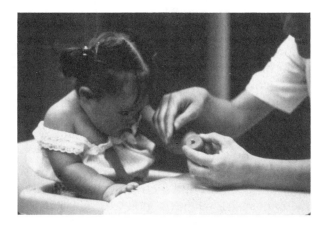

tween your child's hands. Put your own hands on top of the child's hands to convey the feeling of holding firmly and with pressure. Then show the child how the alternate release and firm grasp differ. Augment this experience by consistently giving directions like "hold" or "let go." You may also try to put your child's hands on a stick and then demonstrate how one hand alternately releases the grasp while the other one maintains it. This "trick" often seems to speed up the emergence of the skill of transferring an object from one hand to the other.

The use of fingers as separate units, rather than moving all fingers simultaneously, should also be encouraged. The index finger may be used for poking, sticking into a hole, hitting the key of a piano, or pushing a button. Guide your child's hand holding a peg or a key ring between three fingers. Provide experience in crumpling paper or throwing a block. These are only a few of the activities that can be practiced to avoid unnecessary delay in the acquisition of more advanced fine motor skills. During play, finger and hand movements should be carefully observed. Guide your child through the correct movement patterns. This will serve as a good model for more independent fine motor activities.

Normally, an infant learns fairly quickly that an object held in the hand can also be dropped. Children who develop more slowly seem to want to hold on to objects for more extended time periods and do not want to let go. Therefore, they have to be motivated and shown how to open their fingers to let a block or small ball drop. When a toy is dropped into a metal container rather than into a carton or plastic box, the child can hear the resulting sound. You should reward the child then, and reinforce this action by showing pleasure when the object is released. Encouraging your child to hand you a toy or a piece of food is another way to teach the child how to open the hand. Such activities can also be a valuable early experience in sharing. Verbal cues such as "please give me," "thank you," or "take it" should be used simultaneously with gestures to stimulate the use of language.

Once a child has learned to hold and to release, practice in throwing should begin. Most children start throwing without really being conscious of their action. The arm may be swung about and an object released, landing, to the surprise of the child, on the floor. You may want to pick up the toy and hand it back to the child, who now experiences pleasure in repeating the act. Throwing is a rich learning experience for a child. Gross and fine movements of the upper limbs are involved, and eye-hand coordination is established. Concepts of cause and effect and of basic spatial relationships may have their roots in such early play experiences. Therefore, encourage your child to throw, in preparation for more structured and complex ball play.

Parents of children with Down syndrome are often concerned because objects may be thrown around indiscriminately. Your child may not be ready to distinguish what should and should not be thrown. Breakable things should be removed until your child can differentiate between objects appropriate for throwing and those that are "no-no's." If such situations are handled with effective and persistent discipline, then random throwing can be stopped without depriving a child of the opportunity to practice ball play. By now your child may have progressed to the stage where objects that move are followed with interest, particularly when they move away or come closer. Perhaps, the child is ready to find out that an object that is "gone" is not gone forever.

OBJECT PERMANENCE

Jean Piaget, the Swiss psychologist, has stressed the concept of permanence as an important stage of cognitive development. Consequently, his ideas have been incorporated into various early intervention programs. The following are some activities to acquaint your child with the permanence of objects:

1. Playing peek-a-boo: Cover the child's face with your hand or a cloth, then let the child pull the cloth away or remove your hand and say "peek-a-boo"; or you can hide behind a door, furniture, or curtains and then reappear. You may also put the child's own hands over his or her eyes to play peek-a-boo.
2. Hide-and-seek games: Put your hand over a toy to hide and rediscover it. Attach a toy to a string, let the toy drop over the edge of the table, then retrieve the toy by pulling the string. Hide a toy under a pillow or box and show the child how to find it. Roll a ball under a table or chair and let the child look for it.

EFFECTIVE PLAY

A physical therapist, occupational therapist, or child development specialist may be of considerable help in evaluating your child's play to help you play effectively with the child. Such a professional can provide suggestions for the correct choice and use of toys and other materials to enrich your child's learning experiences and to improve his or her fine motor skills. It is more important to observe and understand the way a young child manipulates objects and plays with them than to be preoccupied with how your child's performance rates in comparison to that of another individual or group of children. Many diverse aspects of children's play influence their total performance. Interest, dexterity, muscle strength, attention span, and experience are only a few of the factors that can make the outcome of an event a success or failure.

With appropriate support and assistance, a child with developmental delay will become increasingly interested in more demanding tasks, so long as these tasks are presented in a way that gives the child a feeling of enjoyment and success. Action toys are preferable to those that may have educational value but do not provide sufficient excitement and fun. Your child's attempts at playing should always result in some tangible and visible change brought about by his or her own effort—for instance, if he or she pushes a button, a Jack jumps out of the box, or a pocketbook when opened contains lovely "treasures" inside.

It is a good idea to present your child with only one or two toys at a time, while the rest of the toys are kept in a closet (or toy chest, for example) that the child has seen being opened and closed. Sometime later, the toys can be exchanged for different ones. By doing this, the child is introduced at an early age to an organized scheme with some order, sequence, and impulse control. This does not occur in a situation where too many interesting things are presented at once and the child is not mature enough to make a choice, causing the child to flit from one toy to another without benefiting from any of them.

Few things enchant a young child more than the discovery of a cabinet, toy box, or drawer. Parents should provide such places but make them a learning experience, such as keeping the closet or drawer closed when not in use, putting toys back in place, and helping the child choose toys to be used immediately but letting the child know there is an option to exchange them later.

These kinds of experiences also aid verbal and cognitive learning in a mediated situation where the parent helps the child to identify the desired toy ("Do you want the big or small truck?"), to introduce numbers ("one toy . . . one more toy . . . now you have two toys") or sharing ("Pick a toy to play with Bobby").

Given other needs and demands, you may not have much time to play with your child. Therefore, learn how to use your time most effectively. Sit down to play when your time and mind are really free, if only for a short period. Devote the time to one play activity rather than to several. Think ahead and plan what it is you want your child to learn in a given situation. Break the activity down into many smaller parts.

Praise successes, small as they may be. Use frequent repetitions, but change them in minor ways, thus adding to the previous experiences. Always stop when you notice that the child is getting bored, and replace the activity with a new and more challenging one, if at all possible. Do not be content to see your child sit for hours and play with the same toy!

It is important to give children with developmental handicaps ample opportunity to play with nonhandicapped children. If there are brothers or sisters and their friends in the household, such interaction will often occur spontaneously. But even then, adults may mediate by participating at times in play situations, thus helping the special child to be a real partner rather than a passive observer. The adult can mediate through physical guidance or by shaping the environment, can intervene unobtrusively to develop specific strategies, can arbitrate personal relationships within the group to better integrate the special child, and can model problem solving behavior. Children with Down syndrome are often more comfortable in a group of younger participants. Chronological age should therefore not be a deciding factor in the choice of playmates, but, rather, the child's developmental level, personality, and interests.

A parent, older sibling or any adult can set the scene for many play activities that promote social and cognitive skill developments, that encourage imaginary and pretend play, that evoke self-talk by impersonating dolls and creatures, and that transfer previously acquired knowledge. A few play activities may serve as examples: taking a doll to a fast-food restaurant, in which the child engages aspects of making choices, ordering, serving the food, consuming it, and paying the bill; a visit to the zoo—imitating or creating animal movements and behavior; setting up different types of stores such as a bakery, candy store, or hat store; and acting out a story that is being read or that has been previously read using gestures, movements, and basic language.

Most young children spontaneously engage in such play and games, as they are constantly exposed to identical real life experiences. The child with Down syndrome may not process the available information as readily as other children do. Mediation in situations such as make believe or role playing helps the youngster to improve his or her sensorimotor skills while learning in less competitive and less speed-oriented surroundings. The child is thus aided to adapt gradually to the more demanding real world. Finally, parents should not forget that they help their child most by being a child, too, for a while at least, and sharing the joy of playing.

Feeding the Young Child

Elizabeth Zausmer
and
Siegfried M. Pueschel

Fortunately, most children with Down syndrome do not have major feeding problems. The reflexes that involve sucking and swallowing are usually well developed at birth and are present long before the baby is born. Sucking and swallowing mechanisms involve structures of the mouth and throat, including the tongue, palate, cheeks, and lips. A stimulus to the mouth such as touch or taste usually will elicit a sucking motion that is well coordinated with swallowing.

Some infants, however, may have initial difficulties with sucking and swallowing, and later with biting and chewing. These children will need some assistance, and their parents will require special instruction in techniques of positioning and handling the child during feeding. There are several reasons why some children with Down syndrome may encounter difficulties with feeding during the first few months of life:

1. Often there is decreased muscle tone of the muscles surrounding the mouth. Therefore, some babies—in particular, prematurely born infants—may suck poorly. Later, when solid food is introduced, there may be difficulties in moving the food from the front to the back of the mouth or from one side to the other.
2. Some children tend to keep the mouth open, which may further impede transporting of food to the back of the mouth.
3. The roof of the mouth (palate) is usually narrow and short.
4. Some children have poor coordination of the muscles of the tongue and throat.
5. The overall delay in the development of infants with Down syndrome may lead to difficulties in feeding.

For these reasons, parents may need advice and assistance from a pediatrician, physical or occupational therapist, nurse, nutritionist, speech therapist, or other child development professional who is knowledgeable in feeding problems of handicapped children. After careful evaluation of the baby's feeding difficulties, the parents should be given instructions, demonstrations, and supervised practice in techniques to help obtain appropriate and effective patterns of sucking, swallowing, chewing, and, eventually, self-feeding. Techniques in positioning and handling the infant during feeding, as well as psychological and environmental aspects, will need to be discussed with the parents.

It is important that during feeding the infant be held in an upright or half upright position with the head well supported. Feeding an infant who is lying on the back or sitting with the head tilted backward should be avoided, since it might cause the child to choke or to aspirate. Propping the bottle or using a bottle holder is another undesirable practice. As a mother or father feeds the infant, the

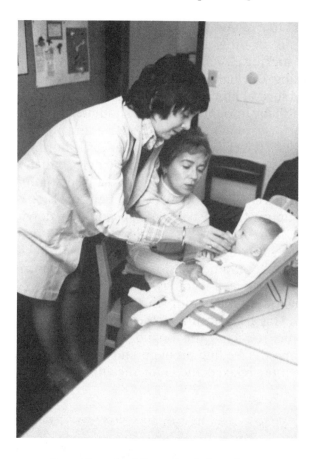

parent usually enjoys holding the baby close, supporting the baby's head with one arm. Both caregiver and infant should be in a comfortable position.

We do not agree with some professionals who discourage mothers from breast-feeding the infant with Down syndrome. If the parents prefer breast-feeding, if the infant is able to suck well, and if there are no other serious medical problems, an infant with Down syndrome can be breast-fed like any other newborn.

If the baby is bottle-fed, the bottle should be held in a

position that allows the neck of the bottle to remain filled with milk or other liquids. Since a steady flow of milk makes sucking easier, one should prevent the nipple from collapsing. During feedings, the infant should be permitted to burp several times. To do this, the parent might want to hold the baby upright against the shoulder or lean the baby slightly forward while being fed in a sitting position. If the baby's suck is weak or the infant tires easily during feeding, one might enlarge slightly the nipple hole so that the milk will flow easier. At times sucking can be stimulated by feeding in a circular motion, occasionally pressing with the nipple upward on the baby's palate and then down on the tongue. On occasion, a nipple for premature infants, which is softer and longer, may be used for babies with weak muscles. Sometimes, mothers might want to use a pacifier in between feedings, which will help to improve sucking by strengthening the muscles of the lips and cheeks. This also encourages the infant to close the lips and to practice retracting the tongue. Gradually, the infant will overcome the feeding problem and the parents and child will be more relaxed and enjoy mealtime together. After a

few months, the child's hands can be placed on the bottle to encourage holding it.

If the child with Down syndrome keeps the mouth open or the tongue protrudes during feeding, swallowing will be impaired. Since sucking and swallowing difficulties are often related, the suggestions just mentioned also will improve the baby's swallowing. Should swallowing difficulties continue, it is advisable to ask for professional assistance; sometimes a feeding evaluation may be indicated.

Usually between the 4th and 6th months, solid foods are introduced in the baby's diet. Many infants with Down syndrome have no difficulty taking solid food from a spoon. Some babies, however, are unable to transfer the food to the back of the mouth. Often the tongue will push the food out. This can sometimes be prevented by placing the spoon on the tongue with some downward pressure. By simultaneously gently pressing the infant's upper lip down and the chin up, the child gradually acquires the sensorimotor experience of mouth closure. The choice of the shape and the size of the spoon, the pressure and direction used for placement of the spoon into the child's mouth, as well as the volume and texture of the food, are important factors in the initial phase of spoon-feeding.

Often parents are afraid that the child might choke on

solid foods, or that their baby will be unable to handle finger foods when the teeth have not yet erupted. However, it is important that such foods be offered the young child to get him or her used to different textures and to encourage use of gums, tongue, and jaws in a coordinated chewing motion. Strained baby food should be discontinued when the infant is about 8 months old. Junior and toddler foods should then be introduced, followed by table food.

Another important aspect of early feeding practices concerns finger feeding. As infants grow, they grasp objects within reach and bring them to their mouth to suck on them and explore. A cookie or a biscuit can be placed in the child's hand to prompt oral exploration. Crackers or dry cereals may also be offered to encourage grasping (which initially might be done with the whole hand). Soon the thumb and four fingers will be used. Later, when the child is more mature, the thumb and index finger will be used to pick up interesting food items to bring to the mouth.

Exploration through vision, combined with the use of hands to bring objects to the mouth, is a rather complex motor act requiring a certain developmental level. Some children with Down syndrome might not engage in such activity spontaneously and must be shown that the hand can be used to bring rewarding food items to the mouth. Parents should encourage the child to dip the fingers into foods and then to put the fingers with the food into the mouth. In the beginning, the parents will have to guide the child's hands through these movements by using food that is particularly appealing to the infant, such as applesauce, whipped cream, or pudding. Soon the child will engage in such activities without help. Many children with Down syndrome use the fingers for eating considerably longer than other children.

Once the child is ready and demonstrates the ability to

pick up foods, various finger foods such as cooked vegetables and pieces of meat and cheese can be offered during mealtime. The new experience of finger feeding can be both educational and fun, as the child will learn new shapes, colors, and textures.

During the second year of life most children with Down syndrome can be taught to spoon-feed themselves. In the beginning it may be necessary to guide the child's arm and hand repeatedly through the movements from the plate to the mouth and back to the plate. Obviously, eating with a spoon demands a well-coordinated sequence of varied skills, including stability of neck and shoulder muscles, adequate reach of arms, judgment of directions and distance from plate to mouth, correct grasp of the spoon handle, efficient scooping movements with the edge of the spoon, and the ability to bring the spoon to the mouth. Gradually, less assistance will need to be provided, and soon the baby will eat happily without help. Good results in self-feeding should always be acknowledged by the adult through encouraging words or a smile. The foundation of acquiring the important social skill of sharing a meal with other people must be laid in early childhood.

Children frequently make a greater effort to feed without assistance when they are allowed to have their meal at the dinner table with the rest of the family. They should be placed in a comfortable position at a height where they can see what is going on around them. The food should be put in a deep dish to avoid excessive spilling. A piece of plastic material or some paper can be placed on the floor so that spilled food can be cleaned up easily. Initially, messy eating patterns have to be expected.

The introduction of drinking from a cup is an exciting feeding experience. In the beginning, infants will spill liquids, but soon they will learn that the lips have to close around the rim of the cup to allow successful drinking. The child should be in an upright sitting position when the cup with liquids is offered. Initially, thicker liquids such as frappes are easier to sip than thinner liquids. Independent drinking from a cup will usually occur during the second year of life.

Mealtime offers excellent opportunities to combine acquisition of manual skills with social and cognitive learning. Communication skills can also be more easily developed and mediated around the dinner table than in a less natural setting. The child can be encouraged to point or otherwise express preferences for specific food items. Choices and options are thus presented and concepts of sharing can be effectively introduced. Conversations among siblings and parents should include the special child in a well-mediated social situation. Such early intervention paves the way to later social acceptance of the child in situations such as family outings, peer parties, and visits to restaurants.

Interest in food and in its preparation, as well as mealtime enjoyment, are pleasures in life that should be made accessible to a person with Down syndrome. The nutritional value of certain foods will have to be taken into consideration. Adequate protein, fat, carbohydrates, and minerals, as well as sufficient vitamins, should be offered the child in order to provide a balanced diet. The quality and quantity of food should allow optimal growth and development. Yet, one should avoid overfeeding. Since some children with Down syndrome tend to become overweight, attention should be paid to proper nutritional intake and regular physical activities.

Although the rate of development of children with Down syndrome may be slower and they may have needs that require special understanding, most often they achieve self-feeding and overcome feeding problems.

Nursery School Years

Claire D. Canning

J ust as early intervention programs enhance the development of children with Down syndrome, a positive nursery school experience plays a very important role in their lives during these formative years.

We all want what is best for our children and we realize that all children, even the most intelligent, have different needs. For parents like myself who have a child with Down syndrome, responding to our child's needs becomes more complicated, because we have no role models to follow or methods for training simple self-help skills that other children learn almost automatically. Therefore, school becomes very important for us, because it extends the feeling of family and represents community support, extra reinforcement that both child and family need.

PREPARING THE CHILD FOR SCHOOL

How do we prepare the child for nursery school? Since feelings of parental anxiety are so easily transmitted to

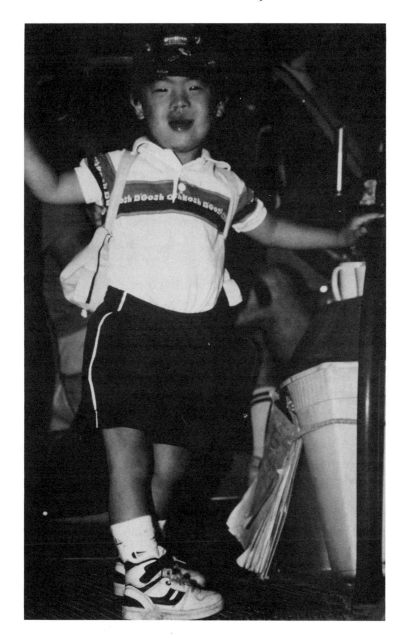

children, we should try hard to overcome our own very normal anxieties, to help ensure a smooth transition. Public exposure is the best way to introduce children with Down syndrome to their community. Through everyday contacts, they become more comfortable with less familiar people. To facilitate this, take your child to the supermarket, zoo, playground, library, church, anywhere you regularly go. Then when you child is old enough to attend nursery school, tell your child, even if what you say will not be fully understood, that you are both going to visit the school. My daughter and I drove to school each day for a week, often just to walk around the building and school yard. We spoke to the principal, met teachers, even boarded the school bus, so that when the day of parting arrived it would not be traumatic. We were fortunate to have a wonderfully friendly school bus driver who made getting to school half the fun of the day.

In some communities you may have the option of a regular or a special school bus. Your choice should be dictated by your child's needs. Some of the buses for special children have hydraulic lifts for wheelchairs and, of course, all should have seat belts to ensure safety. You will want to check these features yourself before your child starts school. Also, an aide often will ride on the bus to provide extra supervision and to help if necessary. It is a good idea to have bus safety drills for fire or accident at the beginning of the school year. Never hesitate to check these and other matters politely but with confidence. Always remember that you are an advocate not an adversary. In all these matters, from the start of nursery school, my husband and I experienced a beautiful feeling of community support. You, too, will find that excellent preschool programs are available, and that many qualified people throughout the community will willingly respond to requests for help.

BENEFITS OF THE NURSERY SCHOOL EXPERIENCE

The child with Down syndrome can learn a vast amount in nursery school. Just as our normal children have varying talents, 3- to 5-year-old children with Down syndrome span a wide range of development. Each child, however, can profit from social interaction and gentle discipline, by working on self-help skills, by practicing gross and fine motor coordination, and by learning to live with different types of people and behavior.

Learning to play is one of the most valuable skills a child can acquire in nursery school. Play is a natural means of growth and learning. In the early stages, children with Down syndrome need assistance in playing. They must imitate, learn through doing, and make things happen. They must make choices and share. Boundaries are placed on their behavior, and they must learn to cooperate. All these skills help to shape positive behavior and aid in implementing educational and parental goals.

It may seem trivial if one has not shared the early experiences of a child with Down syndrome, but accomplishing toilet training seems to me the greatest milestone of my child's early nursery school experience. Recently, a legislator is said to have complained about the cost of programs for the "handicapped," stating that for all the money spent, some children learned nothing all year but toilet training. Another more compassionate senator replied that if he thought about the most valuable skill he had learned in his lifetime, and had to choose between reading the classics or learning toilet training, he would instantly choose the latter. There is no need to comment further on what this means in all of our lives.

With federal law PL 94-142, mandating the education of all children with handicaps, and new directions provided through PL 99-457, The Education of the Handicapped Act Amendments of 1986, parents today have many more options for educating their children with Down syndrome than they had 20 years ago. Nursery school is an ideal time to mainstream our children, a major advantage at this age being an early exposure to language of children who are more advanced. Also, we wish our children as much normalization as possible by exposure to "normal" peers. I believe that the best regular nursery school experience for your child is one that is small. To be effective, its teacher should have a sincere interest in the special child, a healthy dose of compassion, and a sound general understanding of child development.

You may also decide on a special nursery school, a private or publicly funded preschool for handicapped children. Today, signing, if indicated, is taught in many of these schools to enhance children's means of expression. You should make your choice as objectively as possible, according to your child's level of functioning and your assessment of what seems the best option in your community.

My husband and I chose a diagnostic class in an integrated public school. This was a small heterogeneous group of children with a wide range of abilities. Eight children, 3 to 6 years old, were taught by a special education teacher and a full-time aide. The class included children with cultural disadvantages, learning disabilities, and mental retardation grouped together to harmonize diverse and conflicting potential learning problems. The smallness of the class provided the extra assurance of support, in addition to permitting the children to practice more readily the development of social competence. Receptive and expressive language development was emphasized, although lessons were geared to individual readiness in all skills. Speech and language therapy was provided, physical therapy was available, and music, art, physical education, and library specialists all worked together to enhance the development of the child. The teachers displayed great

sensitivity, thanks to a fortunate combination of skill, compassion, and specialized training.

We had to make our decision about the optimum nursery school 16 years ago when PL 94-142 was just being implemented. Special education was still in its infancy, and our choices were the local public school diagnostic class or the basement class, in a local church, of children with mental retardation sponsored by the Association for Retarded Citizens. Today the opportunities for normalization for our children have never been better, and the advantages of mainstreaming at an early age are unlimited. We have no doubt that today my husband and I would choose a small "normal" nursery school, and would continue this least restrictive environment for as long as possible. The important thing is that we do have choices. We must make them wisely.

Whatever school you choose for your child, it is crucial that there be frequent interaction between nursery school personnel and parents. Parent participation should be welcomed and encouraged, since it helps carry over school training into the home. In short, open communication is vitally important to ensure your child's optimal growth. The ages of 3 to 6 are also important years for shaping positive behavior. A good nursery school teacher knows how to approach each child, including how to reinforce positive behavior. Parents, in turn, can continue this work in the home. There must be mutual respect and understanding of a variety of learning systems and options, with all family members working together toward the same goal, the optimal growth of the child with Down syndrome.

What do the nursery school years accomplish in maturation? They open new worlds for children with Down syndrome and their families. They enable the child to participate in a broader world. For a mother, it is important to see her child function out of the home. Too close a relationship will not help either mother or child act as an independent individual. At a time when so many women work outside the home, nursery school can be a helpful first step in the child's learning to cope independently.

Are there any disadvantages to early schooling? Given a high-quality program, the only one I can see is exposure to other children when they are sick. Because some children with Down syndrome are more susceptible to respiratory infections, they may easily catch colds and other infections. As time passes, however, their resistance usually improves. We can all help in this area: when our child is sick, we should use common sense and not expose other children to our child's illness.

The joy of discovery that is nurtured in the nursery school environment is so rewarding to the child with Down syndrome. Eventually, the child who seems to function best is the child who has been allowed to try and to grow. Your child is a unique human being. All children, including our children with Down syndrome, should be given the opportunity to progress to their fullest potential.

School Years

Siegfried M. Pueschel

Like any other child, the child with Down syndrome is the product of genetic endowment, culture, and environment that are shaped by people and events. Upon entering school, children are deep in the process of developing and growing according to their own capacities for maturation and achievement. For many children with Down syndrome, the beginning of school (kindergarten) opens up an entirely new world. For others who have previously attended preschool, the adjustment is not so major.

During the first few days of school, both parents and teachers have a responsibility to help the child adjust to and settle into school. The success of their efforts will depend largely on the experiences the youngster has had at home during the preschool years or in preschool itself. Children who have been permitted to explore their world freely but safely, and who have been able to broaden the scope of their activities, usually have little difficulty making a happy adjustment from home to school. Encouraging children's attempts at independence will prepare them to be away from home for considerable parts of the day. If they have been increasingly allowed to do things for themselves such as dressing, going to the bathroom, or manag-

ing their food at mealtime, routines such as eating in the cafeteria and taking care of their own needs at school will not be a major problem.

In addition, if children have had an opportunity to play with other children their age, they should find it relatively easy to interact with their classmates at school. If they are used, moreover, to contributing to the family's household tasks, they will also be able to put toys away at school and to help the teacher. If they have learned to listen and have been stimulated in language development, communication in school should not be a serious problem. Children who have been raised in an atmosphere that is neither overpermissive nor overprotective, but in which respect for each other's rights is the rule, should have little difficulty accepting discipline in school.

To many parents' surprise, most children adjust well to school without major problems. At times, adjustment difficulties may become apparent in the child who has had little exposure to the outside world, who has been reared in an overprotective home environment, and who perhaps has stayed too close to his or her mother during the first few years of life. In such cases, a step-by-step adjustment from home to school is essential. Teachers and parents need to look for connecting links between the two environments. Together, parents and teachers can provide the security, comfort, and happiness in which the child can grow and learn.

Parents and teachers frequently ask, "Is the child ready to enter school? Does he or she bring with him or her all the important elements that make learning feasible? In terms of physical growth, visual and auditory perception, motor, and other organic functions, is he or she developmentally ready to enter school? Does he or she have the social ability and emotional fitness to relate successfully and independently with other people and with the envi-

ronment? Is he or she intellectually able to gain understanding and utilize information in everyday experiences?
And with regard to language, is he or she able to communicate with others?"

Should all these questions apply to the child with Down
syndrome? Perhaps the real question should be, "Is the
school ready for the child?" Since many of the developmental functions we ordinarily expect of "normal" children may not be observed in children with Down syndrome, the educational program will have to adapt to their
abilities and special needs. We do, indeed, have to ask,
"Does the school provide all the elements necessary to
meet the challenge of educating a youngster with Down
syndrome? Is the teacher ready to learn about the children's problems in order to help them most effectively?
Will the educational program assist the students in preparation for life?

When children with Down syndrome enter school,
we often wonder what they will get out of the educational
experience. Surely, we hope that school provides the kind
of stimulating and rich experiences that make the world
appear to be an interesting place to explore. Learning situations at school should lend children with Down syndrome a feeling of personal identity, self-respect, and enjoyment. School should also give children an opportunity

to engage in sharing relationships with others and should prepare them to later contribute productively to society. Finally, schools should provide a foundation for life by encouraging the development of basic academic skills, physical abilities, self-help skills, and social as well as language competence.

Some parents think that the school is supposed to teach only reading, writing, and arithmetic. Although children with Down syndrome need these basic academic skills, a good educational program should also prepare them for all areas of life. Things like getting a job done when it is supposed to be done, getting along well with people, and knowing where to go to find an answer are perhaps more important than the three R's.

What kind of learning, then, should be provided during this period of development when the goal is to help children with Down syndrome gain meaningful knowledge of their world? If the school approaches education in terms of humanizing the teaching process, if it views each student as a person with individual integrity, if it exposes the student to forces that will contribute to self-fulfillment in the broader sense, then the individual with Down syndrome will be given the opportunity to develop optimally in the educational setting.

It is very important that children with Down syndrome be placed into a situation where they can achieve educationally. Each child has his or her own potential, which must be explored, evaluated, and then challenged. Achievement gives children a good feeling. It encourages them, raises their self-esteem, and leads them to new endeavors. Often the right incentive can determine the degree of effort put forth to accomplish a task. A smile, an approving nod, a few words of praise are usually enough to make a child with Down syndrome try harder. A child thrives on an adult's approval. If the person working with a child initiates a positive approach that the child can accept, effective guidance and learning will follow. But if children feel that they are not accepted or that a person does not want to work with them, then a wall is erected between teacher and student that dulls a child's motivation and interferes with the learning process.

Education of the Child and Adolescent

H.D. Bud Fredericks

T his chapter focuses on the education of the child and adolescent with Down syndrome. It discusses basic values that should underlie their education and outlines the curricular priorities that provide optimum preparation for adult life.

THE PURPOSE OF EDUCATION

The primary purpose of education from childhood through adolescence is to prepare individuals to function effectively and successfully as adults. Thus, good education provides a combination of basic and specialized skills. To provide this kind of education for children with Down syndrome, educators must know the challenges and problems these children face and how best to respond to those challenges.

What makes for quality of life in adult society? Parents of children with Down syndrome are naturally concerned about their children's future. The following goals summarize what these parents want for their children as adults:

1. To be able to interact effectively with persons who do not have disabilities as well as with those who have handicaps. Also to have *bona fide* friends from both groups
2. To be able to work in the same environments as those without disabilities
3. To be welcome and to participate with comfort and confidence at facilities and activities frequented by those without handicaps
4. To live in housing of their choice that is within their economic means
5. To be happy

THE NEED FOR INTEGRATION

If education is to prepare children and youth to attain the quality of life just outlined, it must teach certain fundamental skills, including those that allow the student to be as independent as possible after graduation, as well as those that enable interactions with all people—those with and without disabilities. To interact appreciably with the latter population, it is imperative that the student with Down syndrome be educated in public school settings. Integration into a regular school gives the person with disabilities the opportunity to learn to function in the world.

The concept of integration means different things to different people, depending on the amount or type of integration. *Total integration* means that the student spends all of the school day in regular education settings. Special education support is provided as appropriate, in the form of teaching aides, additional instructional personnel, and special curriculum. *Partial integration* takes two primary forms, one of which is mainstreaming. *Mainstreaming* implies that the student's primary educational environment or classroom is a regular class, although the student does spend time in a special class, usually a resource room. The amount of time spent in the resource room is determined by individual needs and should be agreed upon by parents and school staff while designing the student's individualized education program (IEP).

The other form of partial integration occurs when the student's primary placement is in a special education classroom. This is usually a classroom for those with moderate and severe disabilities, and is referred to as an Educable Mentally Retarded, Mildly Handicapped, Trainable Mentally Retarded, or Severely Handicapped classroom. (School districts across the country use a variety of names for these types of classrooms.) Although the special education classroom is the primary placement, the student still spends some time each day in regular educational environments. Again, this is determined by the student's individual capabilities and needs and is decided at the IEP meeting.

Whether total or partial, integration should occur in the student's neighborhood school. In too many school districts throughout the United States students with disabilities are bused long distances. Many school administrators believe they must concentrate special education services in one or two school buildings. I and numerous other educators, however, maintain that children, regardless of disability, should attend the same school as the children in their neighborhood. When children are bused to other schools, they are immediately labeled as different. Moreover, it is much more difficult to achieve good interactions and develop friendships with neighborhood children if the child with disabilities attends a school that is different from that of his or her neighborhood peers.

The term *integration* sometimes also refers to an educational opportunity that takes place in other community environments. This type of integration is usually called

community-based instruction and has developed because
it has been demonstrated that an individual can learn best
in the environment where a certain behavior must be ex-
ercised. For instance, to learn to cross streets, instruction
must include the opportunity to practice crossing actual
streets. Although much preparatory instruction can occur
in the classroom where individuals can be presented with
a variety of situations through simulation or colored slides,
the instruction must ultimately move to community settings. Exhibit 1 lists opportunities for integration in both
school and community settings.

When considering community-based instruction and
time away from the school building, parents must weigh
these opportunities against the opportunity for the student
to interact with his or her nondisabled peers. If during certain periods of the day the student has the chance to be in a
situation where maximum interaction with nondisabled
peers can take place, these times should *not* be the times

Exhibit 1.   Opportunities for integration

Community activities		School		Vocational	
1.	Shopping	1.	Classroom	1.	Nonsheltered jobs in the community
2.	Theater	2.	Recess		
3.	Sports events	3.	Lunch		
4.	Recreational facilities	4.	Halls		
5.	Restaurants	5.	After-school activities		
6.	Transporta- tion, etc.				

when the student is taken to the community for community-based instruction. For instance, at the junior high and high school levels, it would be very important for the student to be in school during physical education periods, at lunchtime, and at least two or three times when classes change, since the major social interactions occur in the lunchroom, in the locker room when dressing before and after physical education periods, and in the halls. Two other times, immediately before and after the school day, provide additional opportunities for students to engage in meaningful interactions.

Some authors have advocated specified amounts of time for community-based instruction at each age level. I believe, however, that the times for community-based instruction must be individually determined, based upon the opportunities for interactions with nondisabled peers.

CURRICULUM

If we wish children with Down syndrome to be able to interact with nondisabled peers, to hold a job in the community, and to participate with comfort and confidence in facilities and activities to which the nondisabled population has access, the major tools we can give these children are those of communicating and socializing. Table 1 shows communication and social skills as being of primary im-

Table 1. Curriculum priorities at elementary and secondary levels

Elementary	Secondary
Communication/socialization	Communication/socialization
Self-help skills	Practical living skills
Motor skills/recreation	Recreation/leisure
Academics/functional academics	Functional academics—vocational

portance in both elementary- and secondary-level curricula for children with Down syndrome.

Exhibits 2 and 3 list communication and social skills, respectively, that might be included in a student's IEP. Parents should be alert to these skills, the teaching of which should be a daily part of every student's instructional program. At the preschool and early elementary grades, communication instruction should be given primary emphasis and taught for at least an hour each day. Over the past few years, language instruction, defined as learning to speak clearly and in complete sentences, has frequently been taught in the natural environment, utilizing, for example, Holvoet and associates' Individualized Curriculum Se-

---

Exhibit 2.   Sample Communication skills for inclusion in an IEP

Responds to requests, commands, conversation of others
Expresses wants and needs in verbal or nonverbal manner
Communicates so that others understand basic idea being
    expressed
Maintains appropriate social distance during conversation
Touches listener only appropriately
Maintains appropriate eye contact during conversation
Obtains listener's attention before speaking
Gives truthful information
Gives relevant information
Uses social courtesies (for example, "please") appropriately
    (does not overuse)
Listens to speaker without frequent interruption
Responds appropriately to speaker questions
Maintains topic of conversation
Asks for assistance when appropriate
Requests only needed information
Indicates when a message is not understood
Typically laughs only at comments or situations intended to be
    humorous
Uses appropriate volume according to situation
Uses acceptable language (not obscenities)

Exhibit 3. Sample Social skills for inclusion in an IEP

Engages only in socially acceptable self-stimulatory behaviors
Manages anger in an appropriate way that is not harmful to self or others
Gains attention only in appropriate manner
Complies with legitimate requests in a timely fashion
Shows and accepts affection appropriately at home, school, work, and in community
Responds to and initiates appropriate greetings and farewells
Makes appropriate introduction of self and others
Responds appropriately to change in routine
Ignores inappropriate behaviors/comments of others
Maintains self-control when faced with failure, problems, disappointments
Accepts most criticism with no unreasonable outbursts
Typically deals with others in courteous and respectful manner
Discriminates when to comply to requests from peers
Recognizes when it is prudent to leave a provoking situation
Responds appropriately to emotions of others
Talks about personal problems at appropriate times
Discusses differences reasonably with others and negotiates resolutions (with third party)
Laughs, jokes, and teases at appropriate times
Shares own property within reason
Borrows property of others appropriately
Respects privacy and property of others
Voluntarily accepts legitimate blame
Responds appropriately to compliments
Engages in appropriate dating behaviors
Takes part in peer-group activities
Initiates social activities
Responds appropriately to social invitations
Uses pay telephone to make local calls (unless not viable means of communication)
Uses telephone to make direct long distance or collect calls

quencing Mode, a strategy for teaching to achieve generalization (transfer and incorporation) in the natural environment. I maintain, however, that if this is the only way basic language skills are taught, certain effective teaching practices that incorporate the principles of massed practice and overlearning (defined next) will be overlooked.

Massed practice implies the repetitive teaching of a specific skill. For instance, the teaching of sounds to the non-verbal child may require drilling in saying the "m" sound. This may require teaching the child to shape his or her mouth to say the sound intelligibly. Once the child has accomplished this skill, it is immediately assigned a functional role in the child's environment. It may even become the "word" (since the child has not yet mastered words) for "mother," so that when the child says the "m" sound in the natural environment, the mother responds to the child. Thus, to effectively teach language to the child we must combine the principle of massed practice to acquire the skill and the practice of the learned skill in the natural environment, so that the child sees that his or her language attempts actually influence the environment (that is, the mother responds to the sound "m"). The child thus learns that language is powerful and that he or she can have some control over the environment. In other words, when the mother responds to the "m" sound in the natural environment, she reinforces a skill learned in the intense instructional setting.

Unfortunately, in too many instructional settings these days, all language is taught in the natural environment without the addition of massed practice. We label this practice "integrate and hope." Massed practice produces a phenomenon that has been demonstrated as a basic learning principle and is known as overlearning or "mastery" of a concept. People with retardation need overlearning to retain a concept, yet teaching solely in the natural environment does not ensure that overlearning occurs. Even though a child may be presented with a sufficient number of opportunities to practice a skill, the experience may not be concentrated enough for the child to acquire the skill as quickly as he or she might if a combination of massed practice and reinforcement in the natural environment were used.

In teaching language or any skill to a child with Down syndrome, it is important that the teacher follow a set of sequenced materials that carefully builds one learned behavior upon another. These materials should provide for detailed task analyses (breakdown of the behavior into its component parts) of each skill, to ensure a progressive and orderly instructional sequence and one that will be easy for the child to learn. Appendices 1 and 2 at the end of this chapter include examples of a task analysis for a language objective, and for a dressing skill objective, respectively.

Elementary School Curricula

At the elementary school level, the curricular priorities next in order of importance are self-help skills, motor skills, and academic skills. Self-help skills include self-dressing, self-feeding, toilet training, and personal hygiene. Most of these behaviors are best taught in the home or at times when the behavior naturally occurs. Many of these will have been successfully taught in early intervention or preschool programs and so will not require emphasis at the elementary school level. However, if these behaviors have not been mastered by the time the student enters elementary school, they should be of high priority immediately after communication and socialization, because these are essential life skills.

As with self-help skills, many motor skills such as basic walking and running skills will have been mastered by the start of elementary school. However, some children with Down syndrome learn these skills at a later time and may need physical therapy to accomplish them. Many

children with Down syndrome can develop good motor skills that can allow them to participate in sports programs throughout their lives. I have described our son's experience playing Little League baseball. Other parents have informally described their children's success in sports such as ice skating, horseback riding, skiing, and swimming. Special Olympics programs allow students to participate on competitive teams. All of these sports and activities also provide opportunities for building friendships and making acquaintances. Thus, communication and social skills play an important part in the acceptance of the student by other athletes in these sports endeavors.

Parents might question why I consider these motor activities important to achieve before academics. It is because I believe these types of activities provide opportunities for friendships with nondisabled peers, opportunities that may enhance the child's self-confidence, which is so important in one's overall happiness.

The examples just cited of students with Down syndrome achieving excellence in athletic endeavors required in every case the structured teaching of the skill, using some form of shaping (gradually building the motor skill from an elementary level to a more complex behavior) and task analysis. An example of a task analysis that is designed to teach a student to bat a ball off a batting tee and that employs both shaping and breaking the task into small behaviors is shown in Appendix 3. The shaping is demonstrated by gradually reducing the size of the ball to be hit, whereas the task analysis involves gradually adding more arc to the swing of the bat.

The teaching techniques described in the motor behaviors cited here should be used in many educational situations with children with Down syndrome. Not only do these techniques recognize that many behaviors are learned in a graduated way, but they also allow the student to experience success while he or she is aware that skill is improving.

Although I have emphasized development of communication/social skills, self-help skills, and motor skills before academic skills, I do not wish to give the impression that academic skill training is not important, because it is. Certainly the most important academic skill is that of reading. As shown in Table 2, most children with Down syndrome can learn to read. Among the population surveyed,

Table 2. Reading and math levels of a sample of students with Down syndrome (1.2–1st grade, 2 months)

Student	Age	Level by grade	Placement
Reading			
1	6	0	DDC[a]
2	7	0	DDC
3	7	1.2	DDC
4	8	2.2	RR[b]
5	9	2.0	SCMH[c]
6	10	0	DDC
7	10	2.8	SCMH
8	11	3.2	RR
9	12	2.8	DDC
10	13	3.8	DDC
Math			
11	6	0	DDC
12	7	1.2	DDC
13	7	0	SCMH
14	8	0	DDC
15	9	2.4	RR
16	10	0	DDC
17	10	0	RR
18	11	1.5	SCMH
19	12	1.2	DDC
20	13	0	DDC

[a]Self-contained developmental disabilities classroom.
[b]Resource room.
[c]Self-contained classroom for children with mental handicaps.

reading grade levels achieved by the children ranged from 0 to 3.8.

Parents naturally asked: How long should children with Down syndrome be kept in formal reading programs? I suggest that, during the elementary grades, a child should be kept in formal reading programs so long as he or she is making progress. (Progress is defined as the gaining of at least 3 months of reading level on a formal reading test each academic year.) If a student is gaining less than 3 months each year, consideration should be given to placing the child in a functional reading program, one that is focused on reading skills that can be used for functional purposes, such as reading menus in restaurants, signs in supermarkets, or instructions on how to operate a video game in a video arcade. An example of the scope of a functional curriculum (the areas in which teaching of reading should be concentrated) is shown in Exhibit 4. In our ex-

Exhibit 4.   Examples of areas where functional reading skills can be taught

Use of telephone and of telephone book
Newspaper ads and television
Banking
Budgeting
Shopping—ads and signs in market
Menu planning
Cooking—following simple recipes
Job applications

perience, students who are motivated to learn will recognize words that have obvious functional and practical applications for them.

If a student is unsuccessful in learning to read in a functional reading program, basic reading of signs should be taught (that is, "Men," "Women") and alternative programs developed to allow the student to succeed in community-based activities where reading is required. For instance, procedures that allow the student to order successfully from a menu should be adopted by teaching the student to ask for what he wants to eat instead of pointing to an item on the menu. The student should also learn to have alternate choices ready in the event that the restaurant is not serving his or her primary choice.

Although encouraging data are available about the reading ability of students with Down syndrome, the data regarding the acquisition of mathematics skills are not as promising. Table 2 presents data for a population of elementary-level students with Down syndrome in Oregon. According to the table, mathematics skills range from a 0 to a 2.4 grade level, and 50% of the students have acquired no mathematics skills above the first grade level. These data would seem to indicate the futility of spending long periods of time teaching mathematics skills. I recommend that efforts be made to teach students basic adding and subtracting skills. If progress seems especially slow, formal instruction in mathematics should probably cease at the third grade level. If, however, good progress is made (such as that obviously achieved by student #15 in Table 2 who was performing mathematics skills at the 2.4 grade level at age 9), mathematics instruction should continue.

Students for whom mathematics instruction does not seem to be succeeding should learn to use a calculator. Once the student has mastered the fundamental skills of adding and subtracting with the calculator, he or she can participate with peers in mathematics instruction, completing the same worksheets as his or her peers, even in multiplication and division exercises. This will allow the student to remain in the elementary classroom with his or her peers and to have opportunities to interact socially with them (the classroom *is* the social unit at the elementary level).

However, as pointed out later in this chapter, when the student reaches junior high school, there is probably a need to shift the educational emphasis to a more functional curriculum. The need for this type of shift calls especially for skill in use of a calculator. The student needs to perceive the calculator as an essential tool in his or her life, to be used in all money matters, such as shopping, making budgets, and using checkbooks. Instruction in each of these areas should include use of the calculator and should be partially classroom oriented, such as for preparation of budgets and shopping lists, comparing prices of foods in grocery ads, determining how much money can be saved by comparison shopping, and learning how to do checkbook functions. The instruction also needs to be continued in the community. In grocery stores, the student may use a shopping list, compute how much money he or she is spending as items are put in the shopping cart, and actually write the check at the check-out counter. Banking transactions may also be conducted in actual situations. In restaurants students can be taught to compute tips with the calculator. Thus, the calculator becomes a tool that assists all students in everyday life.

Secondary School Curricula

A secondary level curriculum for students with Down syndrome is shown in Table 1. Again, the emphasis is on communication and social skills. It is important that students with Down syndrome have the opportunity to practice these skills with their junior high or high school peers. Therefore, every effort needs to be made for the student to be included in a high school clique or group, since these are the primary social units at the secondary school level. This will be the group with whom the person with Down syndrome eats lunch, goes to physical education class, attends athletic or extra curricular activities, and walks in the halls during class changes. The principal may encourage groups to include a Down syndrome peer. For the first few weeks, certain members of the group may agree to invite the person with Down syndrome to join them for lunch or to attend a football game.

Involvement in after-school activities should be promoted. If a student with Down syndrome cannot play on an athletic team, perhaps he or she can be a manager or assistant manager. People with Down syndrome can be in charge of equipment for organizations such as chess clubs or bands. Participation in extracurricular activities gives the person with Down syndrome a chance to join school activities and to become part of the group that forms around a certain activity.

Appropriate social skills need to be carefully taught.

Too often students are placed in integrated settings with the hope that they will learn appropriate social and communication behavior simply by being around normal peers. Certainly, some skill acquisition may occur through this modeling process; however, all too frequently students need additional instruction to be comfortable in a social milieu. This instruction should be conducted in the classroom, with the preferred method being that of role playing. In role playing, various situations are posed and the student and classroom peers act out the situations. Parents can also use this method to prepare their children for social situations. For instance, a younger student who is about to face a situation where he or she is going to meet some strangers can rehearse with parents or teachers what to say and do when the stranger is first met. This rehearsal allows the student to meet this situation with comfort and confidence. As the student grows older, he or she can be assisted by role playing and rehearsal to cope with more complicated situations, such as how to ask a girl to dance at a school function or how to respond to teasing by peers.

Role playing can also be a major instructional tool for preparing the student to function in community settings. For instance, teaching the student how to efficiently negotiate the check-out stand at the large supermarket will re-

duce anxiety for the student. Another important function of role playing is to assist the student to respond to aversive situations, such as dealing with rude or impatient store clerks. Providing standard responses to such situations keeps the student from becoming flustered. Certainly a major portion of role playing should be to teach the student how to respond politely to store clerks and bank tellers. We know of one young man with Down syndrome who lives in his own apartment in a middle-sized community. He frequents a variety of stores and is known by his first name by most employees, who engage in friendly repartee with him. The store employees have become part of his casual social network owing to his pleasant outgoing approach to them—an approach mastered through role playing when he was in school.

As shown in Table 1, teaching of practical living skills is the second curricular priority at the secondary level. These skills include care of one's own body, care of personal possessions, and, finally, interaction in the community, including the list of functional skills shown in Exhibit 5. A student needs to master many varied skills to function effectively in the world of the nondisabled. Parents and teachers frequently become concerned as the student nears graduation with many skills still unlearned. A set of priorities needs to be developed to allow parents and teachers to choose those skills they deem most important for the student to learn at this advanced stage of schooling. Such a system has been developed by Petersen, Trecker, Egan, Fredericks, and Bunse. This document helps the parent determine what skills the student already has or still needs to acquire, and also helps the parent assign priorities. One of the advantages of this document is that it provides a comprehensive list of potential functional skills (for example, the skills list for money management in Exhibit 8). Similar lists are available from this same publica-

---

Exhibit 5.   Checklist for money management for secondary-level student

---

Uses money on a regular basis
Reads written prices on store items
Identifies which items cost more or less
Takes appropriate amount of money or checkbook to store
Uses calculator to total cost of items when necessary
Pays with sufficient amount of money or check
Obtains change if applicable
Safely keeps/carries money
Endorses checks correctly and safely
Maintains personal budget for income and expenses
Notifies person who assists with budgeting when income check
   arrives
Pays bills on time
Uses a checking account
Uses a savings account
Purchases and uses traveler's checks
Borrows money appropriately

---

tion for communication, social and sexual awareness, personal hygiene, dressing, clothing care and selection, eating, meal planning, shopping and unpacking and storing food at home, food preparation, home and yard maintenance, health and safety, community mobility, personal information, time management, and community- and home-based leisure skills. These lists provide both teachers and parents with the basis for a system of priorities for teaching a functional curriculum.

Work experience opportunities comprise the other area of importance at the high school level. Students in high school should be given a variety of work experiences varying in length from 3 to 10 hours a week. However, I once again caution that these experiences should not occur during times when the student might otherwise have the opportunity to interact socially with peers. Many excellent work experience programs have been developed across the United States, and perhaps one of the best of these is located in Corvallis, Oregon, where the school district ensures that every high school student who is disabled is placed in two to four different work experiences each year. These experiences allow the student to work inside or outside, alone or with people, in stationary jobs or in jobs that require considerable physical mobility. Such variety in work environments and types of jobs assists the student with another major goal—learning to make choices.

Making job choices is difficult for many students with Down syndrome. Whereas most people without disabilities are able to vicariously experience a job through reading, watching television, or watching others do the job, many students with Down syndrome have difficulty imagining themselves in jobs they merely observe or hear about. Until they actually have job experience, they are unable to determine realistically whether they would enjoy doing it. Thus, school-based work experience assists the student to make choices about work preferences for the future. Such work experience also facilitates successful vocational placement when the student graduates from school. A student who graduates without such experience risks a number of unsuccessful job placements after graduation —unsuccessful often because the graduate did not like the job and could not articulate preferences beforehand.

School districts that have initiated such a system of work experience have had little difficulty finding job sites for the work experience program. Employers enjoy assisting the school district in such a program, especially when they have no responsibility to pay students and no responsibility to train. Students are placed in these jobs without pay so that the educational entity can move them frequently from job to job and thus provide a variety of work experiences. Payment for work is not sought until the stu-

dent is within a year from graduation. By that time the student should have articulated the type of job desired and should seek pay from the employer. The goal is to have the student in a paying job at graduation. Training on the job is conducted by school employees.

Another major purpose of work experience at the secondary level is to provide more opportunities for the student to develop appropriate work habits and social skills in a vocational setting. A sample of the type of social skills necessary for a work environment is shown in Exhibit 6. A complete list of such skills and methods for teaching them is provided by Egan and co-workers. The following example illustrates the importance of social skills acquisition.

A young man who was working in an animal hospital and who was normally friendly and outgoing would come to work and would not greet his fellow employees. The employees, most of whom had never had experience with persons with Down syndrome, were acquiring negative feelings toward all people with Down syndrome because of the apparent unfriendliness of this student. The veterinarian pointed this out to the job coach. In investigating the situation with the student, the job coach learned that the student did not speak to the fellow employees because he could not remember their names. The job coach solved the

---

Exhibit 6.   Vocational social skills

1. Engages in relevant, appropriate conversation
2. Responds calmly to emotional outbursts of others
3. Talks about personal problems at appropriate times
4. Refrains from exhibiting inappropriate emotions at school/work
5. Refrains from bringing inappropriate items to school/work
6. Refrains from tampering with or stealing others' property
7. Responds appropriately to change in supervisors/teachers
8. Interacts with co-workers/students at appropriate times
9. Responds appropriately to social contacts such as "hello" or "good morning"
10. Initiates greetings appropriately
11. Ignores inappropriate behaviors/comments of co-workers/students
12. Refrains from inappropriate sexual activity at school/work
13. Laughs, jokes, and teases at appropriate times
14. Responds appropriately to strangers
15. Approaches supervisor/teacher when:
    a. Needs more work
    b. Makes a mistake he or she cannot correct
    c. Tools or materials are defective
    d. Does not understand task
    e. Finishes task
    f. Disruption has occurred
    g. Is sick

---

problem by taking Polaroid pictures of each of the employees and then role played with the student using the pictures, which helped the student remember the names.

Thus, role playing for social situations is a principal tool for helping the worker with Down syndrome achieve success in the vocational environment.

ROLE OF THE PARENT IN EDUCATION

Provision of an optimal educational program for a student with Down syndrome requires the utmost attention and vigilance by the parents. Not only should the parents know clearly what curricula they want for their child and insist on that educational program at the IEP meeting, but they should also be sensitive to the student's progress in that curriculum and make periodic requests to see progress data. If teachers are not taking data on a regular basis (no less than once a week for any program and preferably more often), parents should insist that such data be maintained. Only through the frequent gathering of data can teachers make intelligent decisions about how to alter a student's instructional program. If, for instance, a student is making very slow progress in a program, parents should feel comfortable insisting that the program be modified so that the student can achieve more success. In addition, examination of school data may assist parents in reaching major curricular decisions about their student's program, such as whether or not to shift from a formal reading program to a functional reading program. Many parents may be reluctant to take such an active role in their child's educational program, but my wife and I have found that parents who monitor their child's progress tend to insist on changes in programs sooner than teachers, who tend to be more conservative despite what the data seem to indicate.

Most parents go to the school building on IEP days and interact with the staff at that time. Parents should also feel comfortable visiting the school on other days to observe their child in the instructional setting and especially in mainstreamed settings. For instance, I know of one parent who visited the high school at lunch time and found his son with Down syndrome sitting by himself in the lunchroom. He observed again the next day and saw the same situation. He therefore spoke to both the special education teacher and the principal and told them that he did not think integration was working if his son had to eat lunch by himself in the school cafeteria. The principal took charge of the situation and talked to some youth who were friendly to the student. After that, the boy with Down syndrome ate lunch with a group of friendly students.

SUMMARY

This chapter has described how education may prepare the student with Down syndrome to function in the world of the nondisabled. Educational systems accomplish this by providing opportunities for the student to learn to interact with nondisabled peers in the environments of school, community, and job. Education also provides the skills that the student needs to become as independent as possible in the world of the nondisabled. The curriculum presented here facilitates not only learning those skills but also practicing them in the natural environment.

Finally, this chapter has emphasized the parents' role in ensuring high-quality education. Parents should insist on an appropriate curriculum, should monitor the progress of the student in that curriculum, and should observe the student in the educational environment.

Appendix 1

Task Analysis for a Language Objective

Approximate age for skill acquisition: 9–18+ months

1. Uses words—one syllable

Terminal objective: Student says a one-syllable word given cue to communicate.

Prerequisite skills: Student uses sounds and one-syllable partial words for those words to be taught. Receptively identifies objects or pictures for those words to be taught.

Phase I	Student imitates first part of word. One second later, teacher completes word with exaggerated cue. Student imitates. (Example—Teacher: "Say ca." Student says "ca." One second later, teacher says "t" exaggerated. Student says "t.")
Phase II	Student imitates first part of word. One-half second later teacher completes word with exaggerated cue. Student imitates.
Phase III	Student imitates first part of word. Immediately, teacher completes word with exaggerated cue. Student imitates.
Phase IV	Teacher gives verbal cue of first part of word by prolonging it (not repeating it) until student begins to imitate. During student's imitation, teacher completes word with exaggerated cue. Student imitates.
Phase V	Teacher gives exaggerated cue with slight delay between first and last parts of word. Student imitates word. (Student does not have to include delay for a correct response.)
Phase VI	Student imitates one-syllable word.
Phase VII	Student says word given cue to communicate and to imitate. (Example—"Ask for book . . . Say 'book' ").

Phase VIII   Teacher delivers cue to communicate (Example—"Ask for book"), then pauses for a maximum of 3 seconds. If the student has not responded, teacher cues to imitate ("Say 'book' "). Criterion: When 50% of responses occur without the need to prompt with cue to imitate, go to Phase IX.

Phase IX   Student says one-syllable word, given cue to communicate. (Example—"Ask for book.")

Steps

The following steps are to be used with Phases I–VIII:

Word	Acceptable approximations	Cue to communicate		Phases I–V word parts	Acceptable approximations	Cue to communicate
1.			6.			
2.			7.			
3.			8.			
4.			9.			
5.			10.			

205

Teaching Notes

1. *Teaching Sequence*—Teach this skill beginning with Phase I, Step 1. Then teach Phase II, Step 1, before teaching Phases III–IX, Step 1. Continue to teach all of Phases I–IX with one step before going on to next step.

2. *Concurrent Expressive Programming*—Upon completion of Phase VI for "yes" and "no," the teacher may initiate the program "Indicates Yes/No" verbally. As soon as the student has learned to imitate a word (Phase VI), the "Names Objects or Pictures" program may be initiated while continuing to teach the student to use that word to communicate (except for nonpreferred objects to be used in the program "Chooses Desired Objects Verbally"). When at least one noun and one verb have been learned, the program "Uses Two-Word Phrases" may be begun. The "Uses Words—Multisyllables" program may be initiated and simultaneously taught after the student learns about five one-syllable words.

3. *Cues*—The term *exaggerated* as used in the expressive language programs includes overemphasizing the mouth formation, giving the cue more loudly than usual, and either prolonging sounds (as for long vowels) or presenting them sharply (as for short vowels or some consonants). It should be noted that *exaggerated* does not mean merely speaking clearly and distinctly, since all cues should be delivered in this manner.

4. *Steps*—The teacher should consider such key words as "yes," "no," "more," "help," and so forth, when deciding the student's initial goal vocabulary. Such general words allow the student to communicate a great deal even though his other expressive vocabulary is limited.

5. Note the space allotted for "acceptable approximations." It is not the goal of this program to have the teacher strive for perfect articulation from the handicapped student. Remember that the average child continues to make articulation errors and substitutions through age 6. This program is designed to develop the student's spontaneous functional language, comprising understandable but not necessarily perfectly articulated speech. Exactly what to accept as an approximation may not become apparent until after the teacher has run the program for several sessions.

6. *Alternative Treatments*—The following is an example of a series of branches that can be used when the student is unable to imitate a word. To pinpoint the branch on which to place the student (that is, at what point the student needs extra practice) the teacher can conduct a probe of the branches. After the student meets criterion on branch *d*, he or she should be ready to imitate the complete word without assistance. If not, the student can be placed on the branch sequence again with criterion levels increased.

In this example the student cannot imitate the word "Mom":

Branch	Teacher's first cue	Student's response	When to deliver second cue	Teacher's second cue	Student's response
a.	"mo"	"mo"	1 second after student's response	"m"	"m"
b.	"mo"	"mo"	Immediately after student's response	"m"	"m"
c.*	"mo" prolonged until student responds	"mo	Immediately, as student is responding	"m"	"m"
d.	"mo—m" exaggerates final consonant	"mo—m" or "Mom"			

*For branch c the teacher prolongs the presentation of the first cue (sound combination) until the student responds or a maximum of 3 seconds. If the student has not responded within that time, the teacher should conduct the correction procedure.

7. *Language Generalization*—Upon completion of the terminal objective for any step, the teacher can then begin tracking and increasing the generalization of expressive language behaviors to other settings such as free play, group activities, lunch or snacktime, and home. Whenever the need to communicate arises, the teacher pauses (about 5–10 seconds, depending on the situation) to allow the student the opportunity to communicate. If the student does not initiate communication, the teacher can verbally prompt at the level of the terminal objective for that step.

8. Some examples of other "cues to communicate" that can be used are: "What do you want?", "Ask for it" (while pointing to object), "Tell me what you want," "How do you ask for ____?"

9. Phases that teach the student to use the word to communicate may be omitted when teaching the student to imitate words that cannot logically be used alone to communicate.

10. Where applicable to the step being taught, always present the corresponding object at the beginning of the trial. For example, if the student is to say the word "milk," show him or her a glass of milk at the beginning of each trial.

Appendix 2

Task Analysis for A Dressing Sequence

Approximate age of skill acquisition: 2½–3 years

1. Puts on socks

Terminal objective: Student independently puts on socks.
Prerequisite skill: Grasping ability; appropriate range of motion to reach feet with hands.

Phase I	Student pulls sock on when just above heel.
Phase II	Student pulls sock on when just below heel.
Phase III	Student puts on sock when all toes started in the sock.
Phase IV	Student puts on sock when sock is on big toe.
	Student completes stretching sock over toes.
Phase V	Student grasps either side of sock with thumbs inside.
Phase VI	Student puts on sock when handed to him or her with heel in correct position.
Phase VII	Student puts on sock (heel in correct position).
Phase VIII	Student puts on two socks.
Phase IX	Student positions self correctly: sitting on chair (or floor) with one knee bent up to chest so that foot is accessible to hands, arms straddling bent leg.

Steps
1. Sock one to two sizes larger.
2. Own socks.

Suggested Materials: Use type of socks normally worn by student for Step 1. Student's own socks for Step 2. Chair.

Teaching Notes:
1. *Teaching Sequence*—Teach this skill beginning with Phase I, Step 1. Then teach Phases II–IX, Step 1, before teaching Step 2, Phases I–IX.

2. This is a reverse chain sequence; therefore:
    a. The teacher assists the student in the performance of all phases listed below the prescribed phase. The degree of assistance is usually physical.
    b. The student completes the prescribed phase as described.
    c. The student independently completes all phases above the prescribed phase.
3. Alternate positions for Phase IX would be as follows:
    a. Have student sit on the floor and bring knee to chest so his or her hands can reach the sock.
    b. Have student sit on a chair, couch, or bed and prop his or her foot on another object (chair), then bend over to reach his or her foot.

    In either case, the arms should straddle the propped leg.

Appendix 3

Task Analysis for Teaching Student to Bat a Softball from a Batting Tee

---

Objective: Student will be able to hit a softball off a tee two out of three times during three consecutive sequences.

Materials: Batting tee
Large 10-inch ball, 6-inch ball, softball

Phase I Student hits 10-inch ball off batting tee.

Phase II Student hits 6-inch ball off batting tee.

Phase III Student hits softball off batting tee.

Steps:
1. Instructor positions bat 6″ from ball.
2. Instructor positions bat 12″ from ball.
3. Instructor positions bat for ½ of normal batting swing.
4. Instructor positions bat for ¾ of normal batting swing.
5. Instructor positions bat for full normal batting swing.

Teaching Notes:
1. Teach each phase with all five steps before moving to next phase.
2. If student is achieving rapid success, probe ahead to determine student's ability.

Home and Community as a Source of Social Development

Siegfried M. Pueschel

Even when children with Down syndrome begin to attend school, there are still a number of hours in the day when they can interact with others in their home and community environments. There is at least an hour in the morning while they are getting ready for school, several hours in the afternoon when they enjoy playtime, and more hours in the evening when they can have fun with family members and others. Even more time is available during weekends, holidays, and vacations, so that overall the child spends more waking hours at home and elsewhere than at school.

Obviously, learning does not happen only in school; numerous experiences await the child in the home, in the community, or when playing with a friend. The learning process is accentuated when loving and understanding

family members help a child with Down syndrome achieve his or her maximum potential.

DEVELOPMENTAL ACTIVITIES IN THE HOME

The child with Down syndrome can benefit from a variety of developmental activities in the home. Particularly in the area of language development, much can be accomplished. The way a parent talks with a child, explaining certain activities and events or reading stories, will undoubtedly stimulate a child's communicative abilities. In the area of personal grooming, much learning takes place during dressing and undressing and when children are allowed to handle their own clothes. Having a place of their own in which to keep their clothes will give them much pleasure. They can learn about order in placing their clothes in a drawer or in a closet space. Clothing does not need to be expensive, but much thought should be given to the attractiveness and comfort of clothing for a person with Down syndrome. We should listen to children's wishes and desires when we buy clothes for them. Children will often develop a sense of pride when they can choose their own clothing and dress themselves neatly. Children should become aware that those who are observing them are proud of the way they look and the way they are dressed. Calling the children's attention to the neat appearance of others and acquainting them with standards of dress will help them develop self-awareness.

Children also need to be instructed in personal hygiene in daily teeth brushing, in washing their hands, in combing or brushing their hair, and in cleaning or shining their shoes. Children with Down syndrome are much better accepted in society when they conform to general standards of cleanliness, have appropriate hairstyles, and wear proper attire.

Parents can, in addition, help children with Down syndrome with their emotional needs. Like any child, they need love, attention, and acceptance. They need an environment in which they can grow up securely, where they can develop self-esteem and independence. If children feel good about themselves, if they have self-confidence, and if they can experience success, however small and insignificant it may seem, it will be very important for their self-image. If parents have a positive perception of their children, it will be sensed by them and they will feel loved and accepted. Emotional well-being is of utmost importance in the development of any child, but even more so for the child with Down syndrome.

Another area in which parents can have a definite positive influence is that of the development of independence. The striving for self-reliance is a salient feature in the maturational process of the child with Down syndrome. It is important in the development of children's self-esteem for them to feel satisfaction and accomplishment when they do something by themselves. Therefore, we might want to present situations that are not too difficult and that offer the possibility for a child to achieve success. Complicated situations only lead to frustration. This does not mean that children with Down syndrome never should be exposed to new and challenging circumstances. Sometimes a task may take many attempts and patient encouragement, but finally, when the task is accomplished, the child will feel extreme satisfaction.

Parents often ask about discipline. Generally speaking, discipline should be part of the normal upbringing of any child. It is important, however, that discipline be applied gently and consistently both at home and in school so that a child with Down syndrome understands that both environments have the same standards. Children's social behavior is important in determining their chances in life. Appropriate social behavior is directly related to an individual's acceptance in society and to future vocational success. Thus, children learn responsibility and develop a sense of order when limits are established and standards set.

DEVELOPMENTAL ACTIVITIES IN THE COMMUNITY

Exploring the world beyond home and school can provide numerous exciting learning experiences. While walking in the neighborhood or driving down a road, children will need to learn about traffic and about the dangers involved in being out on the street. For instance, they must learn that traffic lights turning red mean STOP, and that green means GO. Children also need to know the motions used by a police officer or school patrol to signal STOP or GO. Simple games with one child acting as a police officer or directing traffic, either with a whistle, hand motions, or red and green paper signals, can help your children fix these signals firmly in their minds.

Since crossing the street can be dangerous, children need to be instructed to watch for hazards. They will need to know when, where, and how to cross the street. They have to be taught to look in both directions before crossing, and that certain striped areas tell where to cross the streets more safely. They need to know that they cannot run diagonally across a street without looking left and right. The dangers of traffic both on city streets and on rural highways make it vital that children understand traffic symbols at an early age.

While in the street, children may notice streetcars or big buses. They will have to learn about both, because one day they might want to go to work by public transportation. Upon entering the bus they will have to be polite, letting some people go first or helping others who have difficulty climbing into the bus. They will also have to know how to give the conductor (or the money machine) the correct fare. Many things can be learned on the bus, including how to behave in public and how to get around in the city. Riding on a streetcar, bus, subway, or train can

also be lots of fun for children, bringing them many new sights and experiences. For instance, they might learn what a bridge is and what tunnels are for, while at the same time discovering a new world as they observe hectic city life.

Eating out in a restaurant is another suitable occasion for learning, particularly in the area of social behaviors. At first, the child will have to be prepared for these occasions. If family members give good examples, the child will follow suit and will imitate such behavior. Usually, children with Down syndrome have good table manners if a pattern is set for them.

To live in society, children with Down syndrome have to achieve a degree of competence in social living. They must learn how to behave in the outside world and how to relate to people, whether, for example, in a restaurant, neighborhood park, museum, or sports arena. They must learn to respect the rights and property of others and to tolerate behaviors of others in family, neighborhood, and community. If they know how to behave in society, others will feel comfortable relating to them. Children with

Down syndrome usually do not have difficulty relating to people in a friendly and outgoing fashion. Sometimes they might be too cordial, however. Teaching children with Down syndrome appropriate social behaviors, including "not talking to strangers," will make their life more enjoyable and increase their chances for acceptance in the community.

Neighbors play an important part in the child's efforts to socialize in the community. Parents should introduce their child with Down syndrome to neighbors proudly as an integral part of the family. When parents transmit their own pride in having this child, their neighbors will look upon the child in the same way. Children with Down syndrome should be taught to greet neighbors politely and cheerfully. They also should be taught that they can help their neighbors.

Although socializing is an important aspect in the child's life, they should also learn to be alone some of the day and to entertain themselves. Quiet times are also growing times. It is at such times that children may assimilate ideas they have gained and try out new things for themselves. The child should have appropriate toys and materials to use so that quiet periods will not be boring or lead to self-stimulating behaviors. We all need time to ourselves, and children with Down syndrome are no exception. We should respect their desire to be by themselves and not interpret it as withdrawn or as antisocial behavior. In this regard, as in the other measures of assistance discussed here, we are helping our children prepare for life.

Recreation

Scott Weaver
and
Claire D. Canning

 Because your child has an average of over 60 hours per week of free time, it is obvious that recreation plays a vital role in his or her life. Recreation can be defined as activity carried on during one's free time, primarily for fun. It is also recognized as an important means of learning and as a key element in the development of children with Down syndrome.

Your child can realize bountiful benefits through participating in recreational activities. Such activities can offer, among other advantages:

A sense of accomplishment
Body awareness
Physical and mental challenges
Improved self-esteem
Community involvement
An opportunity to compete
Creative expression
A chance to make new friends
Entertainment

Exercise
A feeling of belonging
An opportunity to find new talents
Improved sports skills
Development of muscle tone and coordination
An outlet for emotions
Participation with others toward a common goal
Relaxation
Development of social skills
And most importantly, fun

The child's earliest recreation begins with socialization. Your child will want to go outdoors and play with other children. You may want to begin by inviting children into your home to play a specific game and maybe have a tea party. Perhaps on a rainy day you can invite your child's friends to your home to have lunch or to be read a favorite story.

Most children love to play school, color, paint, and do simple papers. At first your child with Down syndrome may need you to be an important part of playing school, but soon you may leave the children and rather than be the teacher, as the children assume more independence, become the principal who drops in occasionally to check on

the progress of the classroom! Some children with Down syndrome are quite independent, whereas others need help in making plans for play in their early years.

Music is a wonderful form of recreation to be enjoyed alone or to be shared. Many children with Down syndrome have a tremendous sense of rhythm. If we can develop this through listening to music and finding a patient and compassionate music teacher, we are developing fine motor skills as well as giving our child a love and appreciation of all types of music. Music can be a marvellous companion when we are alone, and our children have the ability to love Beethoven as much as Stevie Wonder or the New Kids on the Block. For example, drums are an exciting accompaniment to favorite tapes when a child is feeling happy, but they can also be a great source of venting frustration. Do not overlook the value of a simple harmonica, or a new keyboard that simulates many wonderful instruments.

Dancing can provide magical moments for our children. It will help them to develop gross motor skills, balance, and a sense of self-expression. Begun at an early age, it is a wonderful means of mainstreaming and introducing your child to the community in a ballet or regular dance class. Coordination and grace are improved through rhythmic dancing. It is a form of recreation that will give your child pleasure and confidence through the years.

Love of the theater has been one of our child's greatest joys. She is old enough to understand now that she must budget to save for play tickets. This year she subscribed to a theater series in a nearby city. For a birthday gift the past two years, we went to see "Les Misérables" and "The Phantom of the Opera." The joy this gave her surpassed all our expectations and added immeasurably to our own pleasure. Our child learned history, music, and theater art. She also knows every word of every song in her favorite, "Les Misérables," and the sequence of each song. We listen to the tapes of these plays very often. They have become a very precious part of recreation in her life. Never underestimate your child's ability to grow through opportunities available to all of us.

Do not overlook membership in your local children's museum, and later, in your local art museum. Tours of special exhibits can be arranged for your child's class. I never cease to be amazed at the information and knowledge our children with Down syndrome retain from these meaningful visits. You may even want to enroll with your child in an occasional class at the museum. As an outgrowth of interest in art, we obtained tickets for the Claude Monet exhibit at the Boston Museum of Fine Arts, and our child looked forward to this with great enthusiasm and anticipation.

As your child develops his or her own interests, you will find a continuing increase in the number of benefits derived from participation in recreational activities. The types and choices of recreational activities available are as different as the children themselves and are limited only by one's imagination. Undoubtedly, there are enough opportunities to meet the needs of any child.

Recreation can be either active or passive, and pursued alone or as part of a group. Participation in sports offers both individual and team play. Solo pursuits may include: cycling, swimming, gymnastics, running, bowling, weightlifting, horseback riding, roller skating, ice skating, and skiing. Sports participation can aid your child's physical development in a number of ways. Your child can explore his or her own physical capabilities while increasing overall fitness level and endurance, can develop muscular strength, can improve coordination, and can enhance gross motor skills.

Because we live near the ocean, the joys of swimming are very important to us, but with swimming pools avail-

able in most communities, aquatic recreation should not be overlooked. For the child who is not so agile, swimming is a great joy because it seems to give a sense of freedom to one's body in the water that cannot always be achieved on land. With instruction, the child with Down syndrome can become an excellent swimmer. This is marvellous exercise for toning the body and is a very happy recreational pursuit.

Some schools have ice skating and roller skating at municipal rinks as part of their weekly athletic program. Skates that have been donated are provided for athletes who need them, and low-key noncompetitive instruction can be provided by teachers and volunteers. It is so gratifying to see the progress each child can make, and the happiness and satisfaction that is derived from these programs.

Baseball, basketball, tennis, volleyball, and soccer are excellent opportunities for interaction in a team setting. Your child can receive some additional benefits through team sports participation. Team sports promote group interaction, encourage individuals to work toward a common goal as a team, offer socialization with peers, and, most importantly, help your child develop an appreciation of sharing.

Outdoor recreation such as boating, fishing, camping, hiking, gardening, and travel can provide countless hours of family enjoyment, while encouraging children to investigate the world around them. Camping, for example, offers a unique chance to develop an understanding and appreciation for the environment. Whether it involves a family camping trip or a day or overnight camp for children, camp life emphasizes an atmosphere of relaxation and the freedom to explore, to enjoy mountains, forests, beaches, water, wildlife, wind, stars, and sky. It provides time to develop friendships and to train muscles and senses. Many children with Down syndrome fit well into a camp with "normal" children, while others might feel better attending camps for children with handicaps. Both you as parent and your child will have to decide which camp is best suited for him or her. Most importantly, the camp experience should offer children pleasure away from home, enjoyment of nature, and the company of many new friends.

Arts and crafts can also offer a wide range of recreational activities. Crafts can include leather and wood craft, weaving, sewing, and creating designs from assorted materials. Drawing, painting, and playing with clay are some of the artistic ventures children with Down syndrome will enjoy. They may also want to pursue a hobby, typically classified as collecting and creating. Coins, baseball cards, stamps, rocks, autographs, and dolls are a few popular collectible items. Creative hobbies can include such things as building models, writing, cooking, music, and ceramics. Your child may also want to pursue recreational activities through social events such as spectating or visiting with friends. For the child who desires it, a puppy or kitten can be a great companion that teaches responsibility, a friend upon whom our children with Down syndrome can lavish great love.

Whatever the children's age, interest, or ability, there is a recreational activity to meet their needs. It is a good idea to introduce children to a variety of experiences, so that they have the opportunity to discover their own particular area of interest or expertise. Finding an activity that they enjoy and that results in a successful experience will make recreation a positive and fulfilling factor in their life. Locating the ideal program will take a little work on your part, but the search will be well worth the time and effort. A starting point could be your local department of Parks and Recreation. Inquire about what services are available. These could include specialized recreation programs, integrated opportunities, or other community resources. Another avenue to pursue is your local school district. Many schools offer after-school activities, intramural and interscholastic sports, and Special Olympics training. Some schools have even made it possible for a special athlete *to letter* in a sport if participating in a structured program.

Your community can also provide a variety of recreational options in the form of youth sports leagues, church activities, and special events. Participation in church and community activities can also help to increase awareness and understanding of children with Down syndrome in the community. A recent trend in recreation has been to integrate people with developmental disabilities with their nonhandicapped peers in leisure time activities. This uniting of peers, despite varied abilities, has proven successful in a number of settings and has benefited both groups of individuals. In addition to encouraging increased awareness of each other's capabilities, such programs provide a major opportunity for both sets of participants to make new friends, develop social skills, increase self-confidence, and learn from each other (see also Unified Sports in Special Olympics).

Two existing programs offering integrated recreation are the Girl Scouts and Boy Scouts of America and Special Olympics International. Scouting is committed to servicing *all* girls and boys, regardless of disabilities. Scouting can provide a child with adventure, a feeling of belonging to a group, an opportunity for personal achievement, and increased social interaction.

Just a little over twenty years ago, Eunice Kennedy Shriver invited a group of children with mental retardation to her home for a cook-out and outdoor games. With her keen insight and dedication, she decided that her guests had far more potential than was attributed to them. Thus began Special Olympics, a nationwide program of sports activities that gives our children a chance to come together, practice, and train for annual competition in many sports. The opening of our local games is patterned after the Olympic Games, with torch, parade, and uniforms. The difference with Special Olympics is that every athlete, no matter how limited, is a winner. I am always moved to tears by the parade and Special Olympic oath: "Let me win, but if I cannot win, let me be brave in the attempt." It is so touching to see athletes in a race; if one falls, another entrant inevitably runs to pick him or her up, completely disregarding his or her own racing status. How very much the world could learn from Special Olympians! They, in turn, gain confidence and camaraderie from participation.

Special Olympics has recently developed the concept of Unified Sports, which assembles athletes with handicaps and their nonhandicapped peers, making them teammates. As this idea spreads throughout the country, Unified Sports provides an environment in which children with Down syndrome can grow as whole persons as they train and compete as equal partners with nonhandicapped persons. In this manner, athletes truly become a part of the mainstream of the community and of society.

Other ideas that are developing from Special Olympics are school partnerships in high school, the concept of athletes with disabilities practicing together with non-

disabled peers, and the Partners Club, high school groups of student peers coaching athletes in many school sports. Having more coaches during practice enables the person with Down syndrome to throughly learn a sport, giving him or her more opportunity to eventually excel. An added enhancement of Special Olympic activities is that they are open to everyone at no cost to the participant. An outgrowth of Special Olympics is a program for small children called *Play to Grow.*

Recreation plays a vital role in children's lives. More than just a way to fill free time, recreation should be considered part of a healthy and complete life-style and must also include fun. Your children's lives can be enhanced by providing them opportunities to have fun, and by taking part with them in that fun.

Do not feel overwhelmed as a parent. Remember, too, that no one must be entertained every moment of every day. A good recreational program includes time for solitude, to walk on the beach or lie on the grass and look at the stars. Our children must feel good about themselves so that they can enjoy themselves at peace when they are alone.

Communication

DeAnna Horstmeier

$\mathbf{H}$ave you ever been in a foreign country where you did not know the language? At first everything around you seems confused, and you may feel left out. However, in a short time you find you can point to things and convey simple messages with gestures. You start learning the names of things, especially the things you need to use often. You find that people slow down, simplify their speech, and gesture to help you understand.

If you stayed in the country long enough, only much later would you be able to converse with others using clear sentences or, most important, fully understand their replies. And only after considerable time and practice would you be able to express your abstract ideas and comprehend the complex thoughts of your conversation partners.

Children usually accomplish this amazing task with their native language by age 6. So used are we to having the tool of communication that we may not respect the immensity of the feat of language acquisition.

CHILDREN WITH
DOWN SYNDROME AND LANGUAGE

It is not surprising that children with Down syndrome have difficulty acquiring language. Since language learning is a complex process, language delay is usually characteristic of children with developmental disabilities. Children with Down syndrome may also have more difficulty learning language and communicating clearly than other children with developmental delays. There are several possible reasons for this, including that children with Down syndrome may experience:

Higher frequency of hearing loss

Problems with the motor movements of the tongue and mouth, with control of the use of the nasal cavity, and with breath control

Problems with sequencing of sounds and words

Decreased expectations of communication because their physical appearance is commonly associated with mental retardation

However, it is possible to enhance the language acquisition of children with Down syndrome by:

Understanding what language and communication are

Understanding how communication develops

Recognizing special areas of concern for children with Down syndrome

Integrating language facilitation into everyday activities

Using informed professional assistance

COMPONENTS OF LANGUAGE LEARNING

To return to the experience in a foreign country, you probably first learned to communicate through gestures and facial expressions (*nonverbal communication*). You may have memorized a few questions in the language, but then discovered you could not understand the people's replies (*receptive understanding*). As you learned more, you began to express yourself verbally in words and phrases (*initial expressive language*), but you may have put the words together awkwardly (*phrase construction*) or had difficulty being understood (*intelligibility*). Even when you had acquired a good vocabulary and understandable phrases, you may have had difficulty conveying your real message (*message content*) or using the language appropriately in that foreign culture (*use*). As the preceding points make clear, communication is more than just talking. Some of its facets are:

Receptive understanding
Nonverbal communication
Initial expressive language
Phrase construction
Intelligibility
Message content
Social use of language

This chapter discusses communication in children with Down syndrome according to three different age levels: the young child; the school-age child; and the adolescent and young adult. The aspects of communication just listed are discussed variously at each age level, depending on their relative importance to communication development. Remember: *Communication is more than just talking.*

THE YOUNG CHILD

Receptive Understanding

Young children learn to understand our language even though they do not comprehend each word we say. We talk in short, simple sentences, use gestures and visual cues, and give obvious directions.

For example, we point to a shoe on the floor and say, "Give me the shoe," and gesture with our arm coming toward our body. Children quickly get the idea of the whole phrase, if not each word. Parents of a young child often say, "He doesn't talk, but he understands every word I say." Well, maybe, maybe not. He has probably learned to figure out what you mean from your gestures, the situation around him, *and* your words. But that in itself is a great accomplishment.

How can we make it easier for a child with Down syndrome to understand us? You are probably doing most of the right things unconsciously now. Research has shown that adult conversation with language-learning children is usually simpler, shorter, more concrete, and varies more in pitch and emphasis than with adults. Several studies have shown that mothers of children with Down syndrome, when compared to mothers of nondelayed children who are matched for mean length of utterance (MLU), or length of phrase, converse very similarly. Therefore, you are probably providing the young child with Down syndrome a language environment very much like that of other children at the same language learning level.

However, children with Down syndrome do show significant delays in language, so further intervention is needed. A study by Smith and Oller showed that babies with Down syndrome babbled a variety of sounds at about the same time (8 months) as nondelayed babies. However, babies without delay put meaningful words in their babble by 14 months, compared to 21 months for children with Down syndrome. Further, when studied 4 months later, children with Down syndrome had only 2% to 4% meaningful words in their babble, compared to 50% words for nondelayed children. Therefore, intervention should be early and comprehensive.

Rapport

The most important component of language interaction between a young child and an adult is the caring, fun-filled relationship they share. *Real* communication only develops between people who share experiences and care about each other. As with all children, children with Down syndrome learn much faster if the situation is happy, fun, and meaningful for them. Parents should be careful not to become teachers so much of the time that they sacrifice the parent role. Many people can teach a child, but the parental role is unique.

Shared Experiences

The foundation on which a child builds his or her communication skills is experience, the activities, people, objects, and concepts that make up his or her world. These experiences can expand the child's world and increase his

or her need to organize that world with language. For example:

> Pam [not her real name] learns that the thing she eats in is called a chair. For Pam, the word *chair* means her own particular high chair. Then, as she has more experiences in her home, she hears the kitchen and dining room chairs labeled with the same name. Her concept of *chairs* becomes something wooden, straight-backed, with four legs, and used for eating. Then she hears the overstuffed recliner in the living room called a chair, as well as the lawn chairs outdoors. Pam's experiences are helping her get a concept of *chairness*, or of what makes something a chair.
>
> Pam gets another type of experience when she leaves her home to go grocery shopping, or to church, or to play in the backyard pool, and so forth. Here she expands her world to include other people and activities.

Notice, however, that in both types of experiences Pam needs the aid of someone to talk to her, to make sense out of the confusion, to interact with her when she responds nonverbally—to be her *partner* and *guide* in the experiences.

A richness of experience combined with the positive motivation coming from interesting, pleasurable activities, are very important for children for whom language learning does not come easily. Family and teachers have unique opportunities to provide such experiences and to facilitate language growth in informal everyday activities.

Nonverbal Communication

Babies begin early to communicate through facial expressions, body language, and the quality of their cries and noises. Adults can facilitate the child's communication and their enjoyment together by treating the baby's coos and body expressions as though they were communication.

Child:	"Eee . . . " (waving hands and feet)
Adult:	"Oh, is the light in your eyes too bright? There, it's off."
Child:	"Ahh . . . " (slower arm movement)
Adult:	"That's better, isn't it?"
Child:	"Ahh . . . eee . . . zzz" (raspberry sound)
Adult:	"Well, the same to you."

Later, when the child understands the concept of communication, nonverbal means can be used to convey messages. Perhaps the child has some words but not enough to express his or her thoughts; nonverbal motions could convey the message.

Child:	"Da . . . Da" (urgently)
Adult:	"Daddy? No, Daddy can't be home yet."
Child:	"Da . . . Da"
Adult:	"Show me."
Child:	(Gets on hands and knees and barks)
Adult:	"Oh, there's a dog there? You're afraid of the dog?"

Children also learn that we communicate by *taking turns* with a partner or partners. In both of the preceding examples the child and adult took turns with each other and changed their responses according to something the partner had communicated. The concept is so deceptively simple that adults are often tempted to say, "Of course," and to concentrate, instead, on direct language teaching. However, the skill of taking turns in communication can help the child learn language from all of his or her interactions, not just when directly taught. (Perhaps you wish some adults you know had been taught the skill of listening to another's communication and of responding meaningfully, without interruption.)

One skill that adults frequently have to learn is that of *waiting*. We seem to become uneasy if there is silence, and we try to fill in the silence by talking. However, language-learning children, especially those with developmental delay, need time to process a communication. They also need to know that it is their turn, that their contribution is important. Children can learn not to respond if they realize that if they wait long enough the adult will supply the words. For example, a father talks, smiles, and touches his 3-month-old daughter. The child seems to enjoy the social contact.

> *Child:*   "Ah, ooh, ah . . . "
> *Father:* "Ah, ooh."
> *Child:*   (Looks directly at adult, no sound or body movement)
> *Father:* (*Waits*)
> *Child:*   (Looks puzzled or a little sad)
> *Father:* (*Waits*)
> *Child:*   "Ohh . . . " (arms and legs move)
> *Father:* "Ohh . . . " (smiles and touches child)
> *Child:*   (Arms and legs move wildly)
> *Father:* "Oh . . . yes, it's your turn."

Two strategies are occurring in this sequence. First, the child is learning that her part is important in the turn taking. Second, the parent is imitating the child's sounds, setting up a foundation for the child to imitate adult sounds later on in language learning.

Sequence of Language Skill Acquisition

Parents, teachers, and others concerned about young children with Down syndrome need to understand the sequence of language skill acquisition in nondelayed children. Although the time in which a skill is acquired may be different for children with Down syndrome, the sequence of one skill following another is usually the same.

At about 5 to 8 months children experiment with vowel-consonant combinations like "ba" and "da." By 8 to 12 months they also begin to imitate the adult variations in pitch in longer phrases (*jargon*). Around 10 to 12 months they may start imitating the gestures, sounds, or short words of those around them (see Table 1, for the sequence

Table 1. Sequence of language skills

Level	Average age acquired	Behaviors	Description
Preverbal	Newborn	One type of cry	Cry of desperation, strong intensity.
	1–5 months	Differentiated cry	Cries of hunger, pain, discomfort, and need for attention can be distinguished by familiar adults.
		Comfort sounds	Sounds made with an open mouth (often vowels) may be practiced.
	5–8 months	Babbling	Plays with different combinations of consonants and vowels, often repeated (e.g., "ba," "da," and "baba").
		Gestural communication	Uses facial expressions and sounds for communication and play with others.
	8–12 months	Beginning jargon	Mimics adult varieties in pitch in longer phrases; often sounds like an unknown foreign language.
		Imitation	Imitates new sounds and gestures (e.g., "bye, bye" word and gesture).
		Understands commands	Can use some gestures, words, and situations to understand directives

(continued)

Table 1.   (*continued*)

Level	Average age acquired	Behaviors	Description
			(e.g., "Open your mouth," "Come here").
Beginning word	12–18 months	First words	Labels important items or activities in own world meaningfully and consistently.
		Additional words	Words are added relatively slowly (from approximately 10 to 50 words).
	18–24 months	Increased understanding; word strings	Rapid increase in comprehension. May put words together without a relationship between them (e.g., "Daddy, Mommy, Kevin, Lynelle").
Two-word	24–26 months	Two-word combinations	Uses two-word combinations that relate to each other (e.g., "More juice").
		Increased vocabulary	Rapid increase from approximately 200 to 1,000 words.
		Improved intelligibility	Only 25% of speech unintelligible to those unfamiliar with child.
		Word endings	Uses ending of "s" for plurals, "ing" for present progressive.

(*continued*)

Table 1. (*continued*)

Level	Average age acquired	Behaviors	Description
Conversation	36–48 months	More complex construction	Formulates rules for words and sentence construction (e.g., "ed" for past tense, "s" for possession, "n't" for negation, use of *to* be verbs, simple "wh" questions, and simple clauses).
		Uses speech for range of functions	Beginning to explain and verbally describe in addition to asserting, requesting, replying, and so on.
		Good intelligibility	Still may have problems with l, r, s, z, sh, ch, j, th.

Adapted from Cherry (1979), Clark and Clark (1977), Leitch (1977), and McCormick and Schiefelbusch (1984).

From Tingey, C. (1989). *Implementing early intervention* (pp. 169–170). Baltimore: Paul H. Brookes Publishing Co. Copyright © 1989 by Paul H. Brookes Publishing Co.; reprinted with minor adaptations by permission.

of language acquisition skills). Thus, the skill of imitation becomes important for establishing initial language, although children do not copy exactly but combine sounds and words according to their own set of rules.

Many of the familiar nursery plays and songs have taught useful imitation skills. "So-o-o Big," "Pat-a-Cake," and other adult-child games can teach imitation of physical actions and sounds as well as the concept of turn taking. Most adults find it easy to play this type of game with children. They should not be self-conscious about the play, because the games are not only fun but teach valuable skills. Similar finger plays and action songs can teach both physical and sound imitation. Nursery rhymes can be made into imitation plays by adding action. Suggestions are: "This Little Piggy," "Jack and Jill," "The Eensy, Weensy Spider," "Ring Around the Rosy," "Here We Go 'Round the Mulberry Bush," "Pop Goes the Weasel," "Row, Row, Row Your Boat," "Hokey Pokey," and "Hickory, Dickory, Dock." These suggestions can aid you in remembering familiar rhymes and songs you already know. Usually the child will imitate your actions as you say these rhymes and later add some sounds. One advantage of imitating physical actions is that you can physically assist the child until he or she understands. You say, "So . . . big," lifting your arms, and then lifting his or her arms, if necessary. You have to *wait* for the child to imitate "So" with the sound "oh-h-h."

Children will also often imitate animal sounds if you make a fun game out of the play:

Dog—"Woof" (or others)
Cat—"Meow"
Cow—"Moo"
Chick—"Peep"
Horse—"Neigh"
Sheep—"Baa"
Bee—"Buzz"
Pig—"Oink"

Again, these are familiar plays between children and adults, but persons interacting with children with Down syndrome need to realize their value as prelanguage strategies. When the child can reliably imitate a few sounds, you can match these sounds to objects and treat them as words, such as "ba" for ball and "poo" for messy pants.

Initial Expressive Language

When a child begins to imitate sounds or words, he or she has made a major step toward expressive (verbal) language. Children learn most of their vocabulary words by imitating someone, even though they combine the words in their own way. However, it is very important to remember that a word or phrase is *not* learned until it can be used appropriately without a model to imitate. In other words, *imitation of words is not language.*

Adults frequently say, "He can really talk now. He can say anything I tell him to." Language requires a child to express a label (a word) for his or her concept, combine the words to express an idea, and then communicate that idea understandably to another person. Imitation is a language-learning tool but not real communication.

Children first learn words that describe simple objects and actions that are important to them. The names of favorite foods, toys, and people are often first words. Sometimes children will even learn a more difficult word because it is important to them. For instance, I was trying to teach Doug (not his real name) the word "pop" because it is one syllable, contains easy sounds, and the drink can be used as a reward. His mother said, "Well, he only likes one kind of pop." Sure enough, Doug learned the much harder, two-syllable word "Pepsi" because it had high interest for him.

Adults are usually excellent at teaching children the names of objects and people. However, sometimes we forget that they need to learn action verbs. Verbs like "run" need to be taught while experiencing or observing the action. Showing a young child a picture of children engaged in an action usually does not make the concept clear and concrete for him or her. In addition, parents need to teach social words such as "hi" and "fine."

Young children commonly use words to:

Name objects and people ("bike").
Describe actions and existence ("jump," "is").
Interact socially and get attention ("thank you," "hey").
Describe objects and locations ("wet," "up").
Express negatives ("no," "all gone").

Adults should check to see that children are learning a variety of words that can be combined later into phrases and sentences. Words should be learned with real objects or in natural settings whenever possible. Remember that the learning should be a *fun* experience for both adult and child.

Once the child is able to use a word meaningfully, he or she should be required to use it in daily situations. Teachers frequently use snacktime to require language for the child's choice. However, do not press the child to say the word if you are going to give it to him or her anyway (such as "milk" at dinner time). Instead, make saying the word a requirement for second helpings at snacktime, when you can withhold the item if necessary. As the child acquires more words, offer several items to give him or her a choice.

Sometimes family members are so "in tune" with the child with Down syndrome that they consistently talk for him or her. Although it is good that family members care about the child's wants, they may thus inadvertently slow down the child's language development. A related point is that sometimes young children with Down syndrome use language only when an adult requires it and, instead, gesture if they need something. You might put an interesting toy in sight but out of the child's reach so he or she needs to ask for it. Try to encourage words *and* gestures.

Phrases

Learning to combine words is an important step for children with Down syndrome. As shown in the language sequence chart (Table 1), they may begin by stringing words together, like names of family members or the parts of the body. Then they tend to use a few anchor words such as "want" and "more" and vary the second word (e.g., "want book, want juice, more pop, more juice"). Eventually they make simple phrases such as "throw ball," "Daddy up," or "my dog," which are combined in their unique way.

Moreover, children will learn phrases more quickly if each word has meaning for them. The articles *a* or *the* have no meaning for the young child and should not be stressed at this time. It is more important in initial language learning for the child to say "throw ball" than "a ball." In addition, phrases taught in play or during concrete learning situations are more easily recalled. Playing with cars and modeling "car go," "car here," "my car," and similar phrases will teach the child to use phrases that can carry over into his or her daily life.

Modeling Language

Children with Down syndrome can often understand more complex language than they can express. Although production lags behind reception for most language-learning children, it seems to be more delayed for children with Down syndrome. Therefore, when children with Down syndrome are learning words and combining them into phrases, it may be helpful to provide two types of speech modeling for them. Sometimes, therefore, give them the *rich model,* which explains the concept and gives examples: "That's my newspaper. I read this newspaper. See the picture of the child. Here are the words that tell me what happened. After I read the newspaper, I put it in the trash. Here, you do it."

However, there are times when the child may need a model that is closer to what he or she will be able to say. The *speech model* will therefore need to be simple, short, and perhaps repetitive, depending on the child's expressive language level—for example: "Paper, paper. Write (on) paper. Crush the paper." Children with language delay may need a simple model without extra words when they are struggling to establish language. However, since their understanding is so much greater than what they can speak, we would not always want to provide them with such a "bare-bones" model.

Language Training

Language training for the young child will probably be done in an informal manner by parents and early education teachers. Since communication is often a significant

barrier for children with Down syndrome, however, they profit by both informal and formal teaching. Parents and early education teachers may therefore be guided by a speech, language, and communications specialist, who can plan, guide, and model strategies for the adults and older children who interact with the child. They should also make sure that hearing is accurately tested and that assistance is given when hearing difficulties are detected. Young children with Down syndrome can, in addition, be assisted directly by the specialist, particularly if he or she conducts instruction in interesting, natural settings.

Sign Language

Language-learning children with Down syndrome can often be significantly assisted by the early use of sign language. This is because sign language aids in communication when the child is not yet able to express desires verbally; it complements the child's natural use of gestures for communication; it helps the child accurately express his or her concepts so that the adult can provide the correct word or phrase (e.g., if a child says "Dah," the adult may flounder around with various translations ["You mean 'dog? . . . doll? . . . down? . . . tub'?], as opposed to the child who can sign and say, "Dah," and the adult then says, "Dah? Oh, you mean 'jump' "); and finally, sign language may assist the primarily auditory (hearing) process of language learning by giving visual and motor cues (children with Down syndrome often have greater difficulty learning from what they hear). When incorporating sign language, be sure that adults are *speaking* and *signing* (total communication). Speaking is so much more efficient as a way to communicate, that most children easily switch to words when they can be understood.

THE SCHOOL-AGE CHILD

Intelligibility

Some of the focus for intervention in school-age children with Down syndrome may be on the clarity or intelligibility of the child's speech. We usually do not spend large amounts of effort on the correctness of sounds with the very young child because our major concern is to establish language and communication (indeed, to do so might inhibit language development). However, to really communicate, a child needs to be understood. After a conversational partner says, "What?" and, "I don't understand you" enough, the child may give up attempting to communicate.

Therefore, with the school-age child the therapist

usually assesses his or her clarity of speech, or intelligibility. Therapists have various assessments to determine the sounds and sound patterns that need assistance. Parents and teachers may use Table 2's simplified chart to screen a child's progress in making individual sounds.

Individual children differ widely in the way they acquire sounds. The purpose of Table 2 is to provide information so that parents and teachers will not expect a child to use a more difficult sound when some of the easier ones are just being learned. For example, Art's dad kept emphasizing the correct pronunciation of "l," which requires precise movements of the mouth and tongue, when Art was still struggling to make the easier, more early developing sound of "t."

Frequently, children with Down syndrome can make most of the English language sounds, but when they combine them into long words or phrases, the sounds get mushy (imprecise) or are dropped. Sounds are produced and combined according to phonological rules that are

Table 2. Simplified order of consonant sound acquisition

Age	Consonant sounds	How made
Before 3 years	*p, b, m, w*	Front of mouth, lips together
	h	Lips open, airway open
	k, g, d, t	Air stopped suddenly
	n, ng	Nasal sounds
Before 4 years	*f, s, z, v, j*	Hissing sound
Before 5 years	*sh, ch, th*	More difficult hissing sounds
	r, l	Tongue slides to another position (may not be acquired until age 6)
After 5 years	*st, str, bl, fl, br,* and other combinations	Blend, especially those of sound combining *r* and *l* with other sounds

modified as the child more closely approximates adult speech. Children with Down syndrome frequently use immature phonological patterns longer than nondelayed children. For example, the child may say, "I wan re boo" for "I want red book," leaving off the final consonants. Or he or she may say "boo sirt" for "blue shirt," omitting one consonant in a blend of two consonants. Speech and language therapists can work on the entire immature phonological pattern of deleting final consonants instead of training a final "t," final "d," and final "k" separately.

Work on intelligibility usually requires individual or small group therapy, with carry-over sessions in the child's daily world. Parents and teachers can be part of the therapy process by encouraging carry-over of clarity of speech at home or in school. Some school therapists set up home programs so that parents can work on intelligibility under the therapist's supervision. Although intelligibility training by parents is more difficult than language training, it can be successful with dedicated parents and therapists.

A final point related to intelligibility is that the child's hearing should be thoroughly tested again during the early school years. Not only is it important for language learning and intelligibility but school success is often dependent on good hearing or on adaptations made for hearing difficulties.

Phrase and Sentence Construction

School-age children with Down syndrome will usually be learning to create meaningful phrases or sentences, although they may have difficulty sequencing words. Their sentences may be short, simple, and use the words that convey the most meaning. For example, the child may say, "I come home. I go to Marne's house," instead of, "After I come home from school I'm going to Marne's house."

When deciding where to intervene in sentence construction, evaluate whether the sentence structure changes the meaning intended by the child. If not, work on the sentence structure only if other areas do not have higher priority. For example, teach "I am going," rather than "I go" only if there is not a need in other areas that really interferes with communication. A possible exception may be to teach the school-age child to use the articles *a, an,* and *the.* The general public often has stereotyped the person with mental delay as having language that leaves out articles. For the sake of negating the public's perception, it might be worth teaching and emphasizing articles at this level in language development.

Social Use

Children use language for different purposes. Initially, they often use it to get what they want, to get attention, or to reply to questions and requests. As a child acquires more language, he or she should begin to describe events and initiate conversations. Teachers and speech and language therapists often do an activity or take a trip and help the child to describe it later. A simple example would be to make pizza with a small group of children. As the activity is proceeding, the therapist or teacher models the description in simple language: "I spread the pizza dough. I put on the sauce. I put on the cheese," and so forth. After the children have eaten the pizza, the adult holds up the dough, the sauce, and the cheese to give the children physical cues for describing the activity. Later, simple pictures may be sent home to aid the child in telling his or her family about making pizza. Parents can easily use this technique as part of daily activities, so long as they remember to describe the steps of the activity in simple terms, to use concrete cues to help the child remember, and to make it fun.

If children are capable of answering questions, they

are capable of initiating conversations. They are not real conversation partners until they do so. For example, often parents try to initiate conversation with their children by asking them, "What did you do at school today?" However, presented with such a question, most children don't even know where to start. They often say, "Nothing" or "I don't know." A child may be more able to describe one specific event, such as in response to: "Tell me what you had for lunch." (If a teacher provides a review-of-the-day time right before the child goes home, the child may remember more detail.)

Similarly, if a school-age child with Down syndrome has learned language mainly in response to questions such as "What is this?" and "What do you want?" he or she may reply but not initiate conversations. The child may have learned that if one waits long enough, someone will ask a question.

Following are some ways you can assist your child to carry on conversations.

Don't let others speak for them.
Don't help them as quickly when you see what is needed.
    Let them ask.
Pay attention when they do initiate a conversation.
Set up some unusual situations and *wait* for them to comment. For example, put your shoe on your head (in the spirit of fun) and continue with your activities until they initiate conversation.

THE ADOLESCENT AND YOUNG ADULT

Message Content of Language

The message or concepts that a person conveys become increasingly important as a child matures. Normally, teenagers without handicaps may be polite to the person with Down syndrome, but they will probably remain in a conversation only if they share common areas of interest.

To assist their child with Down syndrome with conversational topics, parents may need to "tune in" to the conversations of teenagers. Most teens' casual conversations center around school, themselves, and the people they know. They discuss sports (with an emphasis on school teams), parents, music, clothes and how others look, dating, and group activities.

Youths with Down syndrome who are integrated into regular classes have the advantage of common high school experiences. However, even if students with Down syndrome do not go to the same school as some of their peers, their school experiences should be similar to those of other adolescents. They may not be learning calculus, but both schools should offer music, art, sports, a school play, a prom, and other activities. These common experiences form the building blocks of conversation.

Teenagers with Down syndrome should be encouraged to have experiences outside of school similar to those of their peers. Have they shopped in a shopping mall by themselves? Have they gone with a group of youths to a bowling alley, a waterslide park, or an amusement complex? Have they traveled in their state; have they flown in a plane or stayed in a motel?

Adolescents and young adults with Down syndrome need to broaden their worlds in order to have more mature message content in their communication and to be perceived as more mature persons.

Intelligibility

Intelligibility is still a concern for many youth and young adults with Down syndrome. Some school districts have indicated that it is too late to get benefits from speech and language intervention in secondary school. Yet, youth and young adults *do* benefit greatly from language and intelligibility training in one-to-one and group situations. The strategies described in the previous section on the school-age child can be used with success for the adolescent and young adult.

Parents may also need to be alerted to "understand less" of their child's speech. Families are often so attuned to the adolescent's unique speech that they may not cue the child when his or her speech is unclear. One study found that mothers of school-age children and of adolescents with Down syndrome understood about twice as much of their speech as an observer.

It is possible, too, that some individuals do not need much specialized help but can improve their intelligibility with consistent intervention in less complex areas. Listen to their conversations:

Do they speak too loud or soft?
Are they speaking too fast?
Do they always speak with their head down?
Do they always sound like they have a cold?

Therapists can offer suggestions in these respects; however, parents and teachers can often devise creative, diplomatic ways to cue the individual to improve in these areas.

Augmentative Communication

Many children with Down syndrome are using sign language to augment their language learning (see the earlier section on "The Young Child"). They usually progress to spoken language. What about those individuals with Down syndrome who do not develop speech?

Everyone needs the opportunity to communicate. For

communication to be effective, the important people in a person's life must be able to *read* sign language; that is, families, school teachers, and peers must be able to understand the signed communication. However, since the child with Down syndrome can always hear spoken conversation, everyone does not have to sign when speaking.

However, when the student goes out into the community or interacts with persons who do not understand signs, he or she may be at a social disadvantage. Perhaps the child with Down syndrome could have a device such as a communication book to help interact with others. For example, phrases and menu items could be prepared for a visit to a fast-food restaurant. Some electronic devices are available that can play back an appropriate prerecorded message in a natural sounding voice. Nonspeaking persons with Down syndrome deserve a method of communication. Our job is to find a method that enables them to communicate as much as possible to as many people as possible in the most natural way we can devise.

In the early 1970s I was told as a volunteer in a preschool program that "most Mongoloids are mute." Perceptions and intervention have vastly changed since then, and we now know that individuals with Down syndrome *can* develop effective, understandable communication. However, all areas of the United States are not using the effective language and communication teaching strategies that already exist, let alone pioneering in new techniques. We do not have to settle for poor communication from persons with Down syndrome. Parents and professionals need to work together to utilize what is available now and to prepare for what will be possible with future research.

Adolescence and Adulthood

Jean P. Edwards

Adolescence is a time of transition signaling the end of childhood and the beginning of a yet unknown adulthood. Major physical, mental, and emotional changes occur. Although most young people cope well with adolescence, it is also well documented as a period of turmoil and of difficult adjustment. For youngsters with Down syndrome, the challenges of adolescence are intensified. Physical changes are often dramatic as these children experience a growth spurt and sexual awakening. Faced with the tasks of becoming independent and of separating themselves from their families, they still need continued protection and guidance from the family unit. Thus, there is a conflict between desire for freedom and independence and a need for security and dependence.

A SEXUAL PERSON

Rapid changes occur during adolescence in physical growth and appearance. The youngster with Down syndrome must develop a new self-image and learn to cope with a new physcial appearance as well as new biological drives. The attention of many parents and professionals has recently been drawn to the social/sexual development of persons with Down syndrome. Observers have noted that these youngsters' social/sexual needs are more like those of their "normal" peers than they are different. Social/sexual development, however, is often more problematic for the person with Down syndrome because our society delivers conflicting messages and ambiguous demands. This situation is compounded by the fact that social/sexual information is sometimes left to incidental learning. Yet, the person with Down syndrome does not learn well incidentally; he or she needs concrete learning experiences. State-of-the-art curricular approaches encourage parents to provide sex education early in their child's life. It is important to inform the young person of the bodily changes they can anticipate before these occur.

The sexual development of an adolescent girl with Down syndrome follows the pattern of development typical for all girls. She will need helpful instructions about why girls menstruate and in the proper care of herself during her period. Although she may be smaller in stature, the adolescent girl with Down syndrome will most likely begin to menstruate at the same time as other girls her age. Advance preparation should be given to avoid fears. Resources for parents are available to help with specific language, as well as direct instructions, much in the way that parents teach other skills like dressing and toileting. Most girls with Down syndrome can learn to manage menstruation, and should be told that it is a positive part of becoming a woman.

In adolescent boys, wet dreams are a common experience. Boys need to be told that wet dreams are natural and normal but are something private. Likewise, masturbation is a normal response to the physiological changes of adolescence. As it is for their "normal" peers, masturbation by youths with Down syndrome should be a private behavior. Although it may occur sometimes in public, the adolescent should not be shamed or punished, but calmly directed to an appropriate place. The adolescent should be told that his feelings are normal and natural but that the behavior should only take place in socially acceptable places.

Again, provision for socialization and sex education should be ensured. Concepts of privacy are critical to teach a person with Down syndrome, to avoid exploitation; they should be taught early and reinforced at home. Social skills training (appropriate ways to meet and greet strangers, and to show others we care) should be encouraged early. Appropriate social skills are critical to integration, to peer acceptance, and to taking one's place in the community as an adolescent and young adult. Encouraging assertive behavior, buddy system activities, and avoiding contact with strangers are also important concerns.

Adolescence brings other social/sexual concerns. Along with the recognition that young people with Down syndrome have normal sexual growth and development, parents also need to understand their child's reproductive capacity. Thus, contraception and sexual behavior must be addressed. Can the person with Down syndrome marry, have children, and sustain a long-term relationship? These are difficult questions, for which parents will want to seek guidance and counsel. For some individuals, they are realistic goals and certainly rights. A life shared with another person or a deep caring friendship is a need that shows no bias, regardless of the presence of Down syndrome. For some, life together may mean a carefully worked-out marriage supported by family and advocates. For others, it may be life together living with a roommate in an apartment or in a mixed group home or adult foster care home where young people are allowed to form deep warm relationships that provide the opportunity for caring, touching, and emotional expression, all of which are basic human needs. Some other young persons with Down syndrome may prefer to stay in their parents' home, with provision of opportunities to socialize.

The young person with Down syndrome may need supervision in initial dating and socialization activities. It is simpler for parents to assist their child in finding satisfying social relationships than to face the problems that may surface without assistance (that is, poor choice of companions or withdrawal and isolation).

Another issue some parents may need to confront is the sensitive issue of sterilization. Thomas Elkins, in *Just Between Us*, reports that hormonal studies show that about two-thirds of males with Down syndrome have normal serum gonadotrophin levels and might well be able to produce sperm. Recently a report was published indicating that a man with Down syndrome had reproduced. Many females with Down syndrome appear to be fertile and can procreate.

In the past, sterilization was frequently performed on females with Down syndrome. This controversial practice has been slowed through legislative action in the 1970s and 1980s requiring informed consent by the person with Down syndrome or court action deeming the individual incompetent and appointing another person the power to provide proxy consent for this decision in keeping with a series of requirements. While states vary, these requirements often include such issues as: Is sterilization in the best interest of this person?, Is there a better alternative to sterilization?, Is the person physically capable of having children?, Is the person sexually active?, Have other contraceptive methods been tried or are there medical reasons not to use them?, Is the proposed method of sterilization the least intrusive available?, and Will it pose a risk to the individual's life or health?

Sterilization is perhaps one of the most difficult life decisions parents of children with Down syndrome will share with their son or daughter. Thankfully, educational programs are available to teach young people with Down syndrome about their sexuality rights and responsibilities, as well as resources to help parents in approaching this sensitive subject.

With the current community integration trends, we must begin early to teach youth with Down syndrome about parenting, relationship responsibilities, and birth control.

It is recommended that persons with Down syndrome receive medical care with the same consistency that non-disabled persons do. This means that most females should receive their initial gynecologic examination sometime between the ages of 13 and 18 years. However, providing routine gynecologic care to adolescent girls with Down syndrome can be a very difficult task unless a special program of preparation precedes the examination. A full gynecologic examination with a Pap smear may not be required for the 17 to 18 year old who is at low risk for cervical cancer (those not sexually active); however, some form of pelvic examination is recommended as part of a yearly physical exam as a person with Down syndrome grows older. Breast self-examination should be taught as pelvic and breast examinations become part of routine checkups. Mammography should be done initially at age 35 and yearly thereafter.

A Social Person

Teenagers tend to be very conscious of themselves, how they look and how they compare with their "peers." This self-consciousness can lead to feelings of inferiority and withdrawal if youth with Down syndrome are not supported and encouraged. Self-esteem-guiding experiences are critical to adolescence and to the transition to adulthood. Parents are encouraged to normalize their child's appearance. Age and peer-appropriate clothing, with as normalizing an effect as possible, and appropriate contemporary hairstyling are two measures that can lead to the greatest physical attractiveness for persons with Down syndrome. Although young persons with Down syndrome may appear different in some ways, if they dress like their nonhandicapped peers, there is greater chance of being accepted by them. Peer pressure and peer values can greatly influence adolescents with Down syndrome, and parents should be attentive to their desires to "be like" their peers. Eye makeup, eyeglass frames, hairstyling, and current fashions become the focus of their desires. However, when peer values differ from those of parents, family confrontation and conflict can be great.

In his book, *Circles of Friends*, Robert Perske addresses the need for friendship, peers, and relationships outside one's own family. He believes that friends are an affirmation to the individual with Down syndrome that he or she is becoming an adult, worthy of being loved, worthy of life, and worthy of being heard. Friendship-making skills are paramount to peer acceptance and to each person's self-esteem.

A Life in the Community

Previous chapters have stressed the importance of helping the young person with Down syndrome develop skills leading toward independence in young adulthood. Certainly it is the right of all children to grow up, to leave their mother and father, and to live more independently. In the

past, professionals have identified skill deficiencies and prescribed corrective services for youth with Down syndrome as they sought to make the transition from home to community residential programs. (It should be stressed here that *residential* does not mean *institutional* care.) Today we are making a clear departure from the transitional or readiness model of residential services, where the program goal was to make the person with Down syndrome more independent by professionally defined skill-deficiency training. Today the goal is to support people with a high-quality life-style, which translates into a consumer-directed approach. An important underlying value in this goal is the belief that young adults with Down syndrome are frequently the best judge of their own needs, and that the professional's role is to help them gain more control and competence in aspects of their lives that are meaningful to them. This has resulted in more flexible, individualized, and responsive options to adult living that are directed at the changing needs and desires of the person with Down syndrome. Parents ought to seek out residential options that reflect the belief that persons with Down syndrome have needs equal to that of any other citizen to be accepted within their community, valued for their uniqueness and contributions, and able to participate in interactions, activities, and mutually supportive relationships with a variety of people—with and without disabilities—in a variety of environments. Quality residential programs recognize community integration as a responsibility and priority and are committed to helping residents form satisfying personal relationships. A wide range of residential options should be explored, including, but not limited to, intensive tenant support, small-group living, specialized professional foster care, and family in-home services.

As already mentioned, top priority should go toward providing individualized services that support persons with Down syndrome in gaining control, competence, and confidence over meaningful aspects of their lives. Housing ought to be safe, attractive, and integrated into neighborhoods of people without disabilities. Homes or apartments should be in residential areas. Generally, no more than five people with disabilities should live in a single residential setting, and there ought to be an ongoing program to enable the person with Down syndrome to be a lifelong learner. With proper supports all youth with Down syndrome can grow up and leave home—a right shared by parent and child. However, as mentioned earlier, some persons with Down syndrome will continue to live with their own families.

A JOB FUTURE

Many innovative programs across the nation have demonstrated that individuals with Down syndrome and even severe limitations can benefit from employment services provided directly in the community. Today we are moving away from the traditional model of vocational services in which people with mental retardation were exclusively served within sheltered settings. It has been proven that persons with Down syndrome can be competent in a wide variety of nonsheltered community jobs, particularly where they can exercise choices based on their individual preferences. Employment support services should help people with Down syndrome explore multiple career choices and job options that provide meaningful wages and benefits. For those individuals for whom supported employment is not feasible in the near future, it is expected that they will be trained and supported to participate in activities that are socially integrated and that enable them to make positive contributions to community life. The same holds true during times of unemployment or under-employment.

A wide range of vocational options is eligible for consideration, including but not limited to shared jobs, restructured jobs, work crews, enclaves, consumer-owned businesses, and competitive work. All involve community employment and include opportunity both for persons with and without disabilities to interact together and learn from each other in the process.

CONCLUSION

Adolescence and young adulthood bring special concerns and challenges, but our goal must be to assist young people with Down syndrome to achieve control over their lives, gain competence in dealing with community living and work, and participate in satisfying life-styles based on the same aspirations as other citizens without disabilities.

22

Parental View of Adolescence

Claire D. Canning

In 1983, at a National Down Syndrome Congress meeting of knowledgeable parents and professionals, the topic of sexuality was discussed. A curtain seemed to descend on the room, as though we were discussing the unmentionable subject, or questioning even whether sexuality exists among our young adults. Now, having helped to guide my 19-year-old daughter with Down syndrome through most of her teenage years, it is clearer than ever to me that sexuality is realistically part of these young adults' lives. Our loving but definite advice and direction are essential to help them cope with this and other issues of adolescence. Moreover, our attitudes and help through this period, as in all other developmental stages, will immeasurably influence the quality of their lives, so that the teenage years can be truly happy ones and an exciting beginning to adulthood.

The gap widens between normal and special children during the high school years, as the latter have more difficulty interacting appropriately in closely knit interest groups. Thus, it is more important than ever to help our teens feel self-worth and to assist them in establishing friendships and in protected socialization. If we provide a great deal of extra support and encourage their adequacy as worthwhile persons, our children will respond to their unique conditions. Let me share some experiences and suggestions that have worked for our family.

First, I cannot overstress the importance of good grooming in adolescence, perhaps more than at any other age. Cleanliness is essential to acceptance by peers and society in general. Although I am by nature a more private person, my practical side told me that the best way to teach Martha cleanliness was to shower with her. I have always tried to make it a happy time, stressing how wonderful it is to feel clean and naming body parts properly as they are washed. Because hair becomes oily with adolescence, I have stressed the importance of frequent shampoos and of proper rinsing.

Over a period of several months, Martha learned to shower and shampoo herself, to regulate water temperature, then dry herself, and to carefully wipe the shower. If she stays in the shower much too long, I use an automatic timer wrapped in a plastic bag as a reminder that she has been showering long enough. She blow-dries her own hair, and neatly cleans the bathroom when she has finished. I have found that if I check her carefully just once a week, I feel very certain that she is totally clean. We also clip fingernails and toenails weekly. Because in our country it is accepted practice, I help Martha shave her armpits and legs each week. Deodorant is essential. Skin moisturizers and powders are nice finishing touches, and Martha delights in using them.

A nice adjunct to good grooming and more attractive appearance is a well-styled haircut. Approximately every 6 weeks we go to an excellent and very personable hair stylist for a haircut and styling. Martha feels a warm

friendship for her hairdresser, and regular haircuts give her increased pride in her appearance.

Make-up, too, can improve one's self-image and is a fun reward of becoming a young adult. Martha delights in having me help her apply a little eye shadow, blusher, and lipstick when she is going somewhere special.

It is worth the time, energy, and expense to dress our teens with Down syndrome in attractive, current clothing. It is so important to their appearance and acceptability in society, superficial though such aspects may be. Occasionally, her sisters or sisters-in-law shop with us, so that they can keep us abreast of the latest teen trends in fashion.

This brings to mind a story from the wedding of one of our daughters. One of the guests asked me who the young man in an impeccably tailored suit was (the young adult, incidentally, had Down syndrome). "Do you know?" said the guest, "I've never seen a person with Down syndrome wearing a suit before!" Unaware that he had raised (and answered) some questions, the special young man danced with the bride and many other guests and had a wonderful time.

Our special people should not have to prove that they are just as acceptable as everyone else, but, unfortunately, this is an added fact of life for them. Looking attractive enhances their self-esteem. It is ironic that our children are judged by their appearance, when they, themselves, are so beautifully nonjudgmental of others. They truly are attracted to others if they are kind and good, and they do not even consider superficial beauty. We can learn valuable lessons from them.

A second issue that requires extra attention during a young girl's teenage years is that of personal hygiene. If you are the parent of a daughter with Down syndrome, you probably worry, as I did, about teaching your child about menstruation. To my mind, Martha needed lots of repetition and very practical examples. When she was 9 years old, I began to take her into the bathroom with me whenever I menstruated. At first I was much more embarrassed than she was. "See, Mom is a woman, and all women have periods. Someday when you are bigger, you'll have periods too, and we'll celebrate that you are growing up and your body is changing and getting ready for womanhood." We named her sisters, and all the women close to her, and said that they too have periods. I stressed that menstruation is private, but that it was okay to talk to Mom or Dad, or anyone really close about it. As months passed, we continued our discussions, and Martha accepted them very matter-of-factly. She began to position napkins in place for me. Once again, it was a good time to stress personal hygiene and cleanliness. When Martha began to menstruate at barely 11 years old, she accepted this happily as part of the celebration of her coming womanhood. She helps me mark an M on the calendar at the onset of each period, and takes care of herself and napkin changes conscientiously and without fanfare. I have explained that, before her period, due to increased hormonal activity in her body, she may feel sad or tired, but that with new medications available, this can usually be remedied simply. Martha herself has solved a problem that was a major concern in my life.

Sexuality and marriage are also crucial issues to address with your child with special needs. Martha is very fortunate to have two older brothers, two older sisters, all married, and eight nieces and nephews. Her brother who has no children is a perfect example for her that not everyone has a family; her unmarried uncle is another fine example that many people have a full, rich life but never marry. Most of all, I feel it is so important that Martha knows we all have the right to make choices in our lives. When her sisters were pregnant, it was the perfect opportunity to observe their changing bodies, even to feel a moving child within them, to discuss their pregnancies, and to be present to celebrate their joy after the birth of each new baby. We have been able to see the wonder—and the work and responsibility—of each new child. I have the opportunity to teach gentle sex when we change diapers and bathe the grandchildren. It is important to give information at a level you feel your teen can comprehend. In all discussions, I have stressed that the human body is beautiful and sacred, and that no one has the right to touch Martha's body against her wishes. She knows she can always tell her dad or me if anyone violates her privacy. I always stress, too, that our discussions are private and are not intended for everyone to hear.

Now that our children have matured and have become high school students, they will naturally feel a desire for socialization. When Martha first came home and said excitedly that a young man in her class had invited her to the homecoming weekend dance, I felt precariously on the brink of a new adventure. School dances are so exciting to all teenagers, but I feel we must assure our special young adults of protected socialization. Martha's wise teacher and classroom aide suggested that there is always a need for chaperones at school dances. So whenever Martha attends a dance we drive, pick up friends, and chaperone at a discrete distance, sometimes leave the teens for an hour or two, then return to take them out for a snack after the party. Thus far, this has been completely satisfactory for all concerned. We are so impressed with the sensitivity of the "normal" high school teens toward our young adults. They feel so welcome at pep rallies, school plays, and dances, and feel very much part of the spirit of their high school. We have even promised to save for a limousine rental for that wonderfully anticipated time when Martha will attend her senior prom, without us, before she graduates from high school.

I am reminded of another anecdote regarding adolescence and appropriate behavior. It was a beautiful, sunshiny day and the teens at our local high school felt the warmth and glow of spring. One young man in Martha's class called her "sweetheart," and she beamed. At the school bus stop, they held hands, and, ever so gently, he kissed her—and she loved it! The classroom aide witnessed this and felt compelled to feign being angry and said: "Stop that immediately. That is not appropriate behavior for school!" Martha brought a note home recounting the incident, and we, of course, agreed with the teacher that school was not an appropriate place to kiss. It is nice to have both boyfriends and girlfriends, but it is very important to behave responsibly at school. I was delighted, nevertheless, to feel that these two young adults enjoyed a kiss on a spring afternoon!

It is also vital during the teen years to set aside special time for you and your teen to talk together about feelings. Our favorite place is a beautiful beach nearby, where we often take long walks together in all seasons. I realized how special this was one day when, as we walked, Martha asked: "Do some things make you happy? Do other things make you sad?" "Suppose you tell me first what makes you happy or sad," I answered. We had a wonderful, mature conversation, and I have never felt closer to Martha than that day.

Surely many challenges lie ahead. I certainly do not have all the answers. I will need the continued support of husband, family, and friends. But I do know we have come a long, long way since Martha's birth. We have learned that despite all our human frailties, this is a wonderful world, and we have come to know the beauty of so many wondrous people along the way. Our goal is to make Martha as independent and happy as possible and to help her continue to make good choices. She must always feel the importance of love, praise, and acceptance. She must continue to have a healthy self-respect, as well as the respect of her family and friends.

23

Vocational Training and Employment

Siegfried M. Pueschel

Although the process often involves considerable frustration and anxiety, parents will need to help the young adult with Down syndrome move from the sheltered environment of the home into the world of work and toward forming relationships with nonretarded adults.

During the formative years of vocational development, the young adult with Down syndrome must begin to experience concretely the essential components of career development. Through a process of experiencing different vocational opportunities, the young adult can begin to formulate vocational expectations. In addition to identifying specific likes and dislikes, a prevocational program, which is often part of high school education, provides young adults with the chance to begin to accept responsibility for their actions and thus begin to share in planning for their future. It is important for persons with Down syndrome to play as active a role as possible in making decisions regarding their future employment options.

PREVOCATIONAL TRAINING

Prior to becoming involved in vocational activities, the person with Down syndrome should begin to be exposed to prevocational training activities. Initially, each student should be carefully evaluated with respect to ability, interest, and social skills. There should also be an opportunity for students to "test" themselves in many types of vocational activities. Such an assessment process permits the development of an exploratory prevocational program.

In a work-study program, students may spend a portion of their day in the classroom, focusing on academic skills. During the remainder of the day, students may leave the school for an on-the-job training program in the community. The kind of placement will depend on the student's aptitude, ability, and readiness; and the nature of the work experience will vary according to the design and philosophy of each program. The primary purpose of the work experience, however, is not to develop specific vocational skills, but to enable a student to attain good work habits and the interpersonal skills necessary to maintain a job. If in the course of training, specific skills are acquired, they will be helpful in obtaining a job later. Specific skill competencies should not be emphasized at this stage, however, at the expense of practicing effective vocational behavior and adjustment to work.

Cooperation between the public school, the vocational rehabilitation agency, and other involved agencies is a prerequisite for developing a good program for the student with Down syndrome. A work-study program should include a close working relationship between the public school teacher and the job coach so that academic programs may be made meaningful in terms of the young persons' work-study experience. Special academic training, attitudes, behavior patterns, and relationships with co-workers and supervisors should be stressed by both the school and employment staff to assure maximum progress.

A VOCATIONAL PROGRAM

Based on an evaluation of the student's prevocational experience, parents and school can decide together with the student which vocational program will be of the greatest benefit. A vocational program should provide the student with a structured and realistic vocational experience to enable him or her to achieve maximum success. This program should be based on the student's ultimate vocational needs and should also emphasize the development of interpersonal skills required in most jobs. Success of individuals with Down syndrome in the job market is in part based on their efficiency in doing a job, coupled with such character traits as steadiness, reliability, diligence, responsibility, and trustworthiness on the job. A person's social adjustment and relationship with co-workers are also frequently important factors in attaining job success.

Once on the job, employees with Down syndrome will need to establish a meaningful relationship with their employer and co-workers. Many job-trained persons with Down syndrome are capable of carrying out most job responsibilities. They often impress their employers with skills and attitudes they were unable to verbalize when initially seeking employment. Many individuals previously considered unemployable have been trained for employment and have found jobs. The ultimate goal of all work programs is to prepare the young person to function at the highest level possible in employment.

Undoubtedly, the first few days and weeks of adjustment on the job are critical. In some instances, frustrations faced in the new environment, coupled with an occasional traumatic experience that a new employee encounters, can result in loss of a job after substantial investment in training and placement. Therefore, during this initial adjustment, assistance is essential to guide the young person with Down syndrome, in order to avoid failure and to prevent a premature withdrawal from a situation.

Too frequently, individuals with handicaps, and in particular, persons with Down syndrome, are vocationally stereotyped and are ushered into positions such as dishwashers and janitors. But whereas these occupations might be complex and personally satisfying and rewarding for many individuals, they often represent a lack of consideration for the individual worker's interest and aptitude. Creativity and imagination can open up a wider variety of occupations for the person with handicaps, such as a job at a fast food restaurant, basic carpentry, supermarket assistant, or nursing home attendant.

On the other hand, some individuals with Down syndrome might set vocational goals for themselves that cannot be realized. On occasion, parents also have inappropriate expectations for the student. Often these vocational aspirations carry with them educational requirements beyond the student's capabilities. Teachers and counselors must help both students and parents establish realistic vocational choices that are functional and still satisfying to the individual.

Sometimes parents think that a low-paying or unskilled job is demeaning for their son or daughter. As a result, they may deprive him or her of an important work experience and of the opportunity to develop greater interpersonal skills. Situations where individuals with Down syndrome may be misused should, of course, be avoided. Persons with Down syndrome should be accepted for what they are and for what they can do, and praised and paid accordingly.

It is important that through their work persons with Down syndrome gain a feeling of self-worth and of contributing to the community. The work experience is important for every person, but particularly so for persons with handicaps, as it is a chance for them to prove to themselves and others that they are capable. Such an accomplishment will increase their self-esteem and satisfy their family. Society, too, should acknowledge their contribution.

In addition to the work aspect, vocational involvement should also focus on recreation and social adjustment. Adult recreational activities should be made available. The development of social adjustment skills enables the person with Down syndrome to establish interpersonal relationships with others of similar interests. A person with Down syndrome should be afforded the normal experiences of making friends. Parents, schools, and vocational centers can aid in the development of interpersonal relationships by providing ample opportunities for persons with handicaps to meet and get to know other people. The resulting ongoing, warm, human relationships, which are vital for every human being, will also be deeply satisfying to persons with Down syndrome and an important dimension of their happiness.

24

Planning a Future Quality of Life

Siegfried M. Pueschel

Previous chapters in this book have stressed that opportunities and assistance should be provided to children and adolescents with Down syndrome to enable them to become as independent as possible. It has been emphasized that because the early years are of utmost importance in paving the way for the future, independence training should start in infancy; that it is during the school years that social behaviors are shaped; and that individuals with Down syndrome also need exposure to various life experiences to enable them to function optimally in society.

Now, on the threshold of our children's entry into adulthood, new questions arise: How will our children use their acquired skills in the years ahead? How will they function in the community? And for parents, perhaps the most crucial question of all: "What will become of our children after we are gone?"

If we have succeeded in giving our children with Down syndrome the tools to accomplish things in life by stimulating in them curiosity and a desire to learn, if we have helped them develop ways to communicate and to be independent, and if we have made them aware of their abilities and strengths, we will have done much to pave a bright future for them. If our children have been trained to display acceptable social behaviors, and if we have instilled in them a belief in their self-worth, we will have had a significant impact on their lives.

In the past two decades the interest in persons with mental retardation has focused primarily on programs for young special needs children, including those with Down syndrome. This focus is now changing, with a recent emphasis being given to the needs of adults with mental retardation. There is a growing concern to provide these individuals with appropriate jobs and living arrangements, as well as with recreational opportunities and social interactions.

The question is often asked, Should all persons with Down syndrome leave their parents' home when they reach adulthood? Although many individuals with Down syndrome who have finished school and job training may some day move out of the home to form new living ar-

rangements, others will continue to stay with their parents. Many persons with Down syndrome prefer to remain in the loving and secure environment of the parental home, and their parents are likewise happy to have the continuing companionship of their son or daughter. In such cases, it would be counterproductive to uproot persons against their will and that of their parents. Moreover, from a logistic point of view, there are just not enough community residences, apartments, or group homes available at present for all persons with handicapping conditions. Therefore, not all persons should be placed in group homes or similar living arrangements.

For those individuals who plan to move into an apartment or group home, parents have a number of concerns, including the quality of the living arrangement; the availability of food, medical care, transportation, and recreational opportunities; the safety of the new environment; and provisions for assuring their son or daughter's emotional well-being. This chapter delineates a number of these and other concerns that affect the quality of living arrangements for adults with Down syndrome.

ENVIRONMENTAL SAFEGUARDS

No matter how attractive a particular community setting may be or how well it meets federal or local standards, there are no guarantees that an individual will in fact participate in that setting in a personally satisfying and socially productive manner. Therefore, it is important that emotional and social supports be available during the transition process from the home to other living arrangements in the community. Adequate counseling and optimal preparation are essential elements in this process.

It is paramount that the new environment provide the individual with enjoyment; with feelings of being loved, of

self-worth, and of self-trust; and with a sense of belonging. Whereas these concerns are significant for any human being, they may be even more important for the person with Down syndrome who is leaving the parental home.

THE PLANNING PROCESS

Although it may be difficult for some persons with Down syndrome to articulate their wants and needs, they should be involved in the decision-making process relating to their new environment. In the past, many such individuals have been denied choices and have more or less been forced into an unfamiliar setting. Even for those individuals who know and can express their preferences, limitations in their social competence may create insurmountable obstacles to the realization of those preferences.

In planning community living for adults with Down syndrome, one must define the individual's needs and then see whether the community can meet these needs. Like the rest of us, persons with Down snydrome have both physiological and psychological needs. Physiological needs include food, clothing, and shelter, which must be satisfied if the person is to survive. The bodily needs of these individuals thus do not appear to differ significantly from those of the general population. Also like the general population, the psychosocial needs of individuals with Down syndrome may vary from culture to culture and person to person, and include needs for security, for a sense of adequacy, and to love and be loved. In addition, the adult with Down syndrome has special needs for appropriate counseling, for recreational facilities, and for work opportunities. Failure to satisfy these needs may lead to failure in community living. It is important not to overlook these physiological and psychosocial needs, since in the past adults with Down syndrome have often been treated as though their only problem were mental retardation. Experience has shown that adults with Down syndrome living in the community need to be provided with services that are broad and comprehensive, as well as highly specific, if their needs are to be met at all.

The goals of a well-conceived community program should provide conditions and circumstances to enable adult persons with Down syndrome to perform adequately the activities of daily living while residing harmoniously in the community, to achieve a maximum level of economic productivity, and to fulfill normal civic responsibilities commensurate with their abilities. Comprehensive personal, social, and vocational services should be provided. Recreational and leisure-time activities should be included. Finally, we must work aggressively to develop ways to make the lives of adults with Down syndrome more meaningful.

Planning for the person with Down syndrome must be related to the community planning for all citizens, but especially for all persons with handicaps. Various community services will need to be coordinated, in order to provide for the general and specific requirements of adults with Down syndrome. Planning should ideally include both the recipients and providers of services. When total responsibility for program planning and implementation rests with a particular agency, with little or no participation by the users of services, many misconceptions may be introduced. Whereas some adults with Down syndrome may indeed contribute in planning and implementing programs, others may be passive observers. As adults with Down syndrome develop in maturity and social competence, they may well demonstrate capabilities for planning and for self-direction in programs and decision making that could contribute to their own independent living in the community.

In considering living arrangements for the adult with Down syndrome, one must take into account such factors as age, sex, degree of mental handicap, medical and emotional problems, and job situation. It is important that living quarters be designed not only in terms of bed space but in terms of the person's total life-style. In some circumstances adults with Down syndrome may live together in a home in total independence; in others, parents or responsible relatives are in charge; or in half-way house situations, considerable supervision and supportive services are available.

There is, furthermore, a need for educational programs for the general community regarding the needs of adults with Down syndrome. Only by continuing to forge more enlightened attitudes will our people with Down syndrome be accepted by society so that they may, to the best of their abilities, participate realistically in community life.

Epilogue

Siegfried M. Pueschel

We all hope that in the future, instead of lip service, persons with Down syndrome will be offered a status that observes their rights and privileges as citizens in a democratic society and, in a real sense, preserves their human dignity. Society must realize that individuals with Down syndrome are people in their own right, in spite of their limited capacity for academic achievement, with needs, wishes, and hopes that ought to be recognized. The future promises programs that will guide and assist persons with Down syndrome to develop their own identities and lead lives that are as independent as possible. Such optimism regarding the future is warranted only if we retain a solid grip on the accomplishments of the present and build on the wisdom derived from the past.

References and Suggested Readings

CHAPTER 1

Pueschel, S.M. (1986). The impact on the family with a handicapped child. *Issues in Law and Medicine, 2,* 171–187.

Pueschel, S.M. (1986). When the child has a handicapping condition: Counseling parents. *Early Childhood Update, 2,* 1–6.

Pueschel, S.M., Bernier, J.C., & Gossler, S.J. (1989). Parents helping parents. *Exceptional Parent, 19,* 56–59.

CHAPTER 2

Dougan, T., Isabell, L., & Vyas, P. (1983). *We have been there.* Nashville: Abingdon Press.

Featherstone, H. (1980). *A difference in the family.* New York: Penguin Paperbacks.

Murphy, A. (1984). Social service evaluations. In S.M. Pueschel (Ed.), *The young child with Down syndrome* (pp. 87–103). New York: Human Sciences Press.

Murphy, A., Pueschel, S.M., & Schneider, J. (1973). Group work with parents of children with Down's syndrome. *Social Casework,* (Feb.), 114–119.

Pueschel, S.M., & Murphy, A. (1975). Counseling parents of infants with Down's Syndrome. *Postgraduate Medicine, 58* (7), 90–95.

CHAPTER 3

Stray-Gundersen, K. (Ed.). (1986). *Babies with Down syndrome: A new parent's guide.* Rockville, MD: Woodbine House.
Tingey, C. (1988). *Down syndrome: A resource handbook.* Boston: College-Hill Press/Little, Brown & Co.

CHAPTER 4

Jost, D.A., & Crocker, A.C. (1987). The handling of Down syndrome and related terms in modern dictionaries. *Journal of the Dictionary Society of North America, 9,* 97–109.
Rynders, J.E. (1987). History of Down syndrome: The need for a new perspective. In S.M. Pueschel, C. Tingey, J.E. Rynders, A.C. Crocker, & D.M. Crutcher (Eds.), *New perspectives on Down syndrome* (pp. 1–17). Baltimore: Paul H. Brookes Publishing Co.
Scheerenberger, R.C. (1983). *A history of mental retardation* (pp. 56–58). Baltimore: Paul H. Brookes Publishing Co.
Smith, G.F., & Berg, J.M. (1976). *Down's anomaly* (pp. 1–13). Edinburgh, Scotland: Churchill Livingstone.

CHAPTER 5

Crowley, P.H., Hayden, T.L., & Dushyant, K.G. (1982). Etiology of Down Syndrome. In S.M. Pueschel & J.E. Rynders (Eds.), *Down syndrome: Advances in biomedicine and the behavioral sciences* (pp. 89–131). Cambridge, MA: Ware Press.
Hamers, A.J., Vaes-Peeters, G.P., Jongbloed, R.J., Millington-Ward, A.M., Meijer, H., De Die-Smulders, C.E., & Geraedts, J.P. (1987). On the origin of recurrent trisomy 21: Determination using chromosomal and DNA polymorphisms. *Clinical Genetics, 32,* 409–413.
Jagiello, G.M., Fang, J-S., Ducayen, M.B., & Sung, W.K. (1987). Etiology of human trisomy 21. In S.M. Pueschel, C. Tingey, J.E. Rynders, A.C. Crocker, & D.M. Crutcher (Eds.), *New per-*

spectives on Down syndrome (pp. 23–38). Baltimore: Paul H. Brookes Publishing Co.

Pueschel, S.M. (1986). *An overview of Down syndrome.* Arlington, TX: Association for Retarded Citizens of the United States.

CHAPTER 6

Batshaw, M.L., & Perret, Y.M. (1986). *Children with handicaps: A medical primer* (2nd ed.). Baltimore: Paul H. Brookes Publishing Co.

DiMaio, M.S., Baumgarten, A., Greenstein, R.M., Saul, H.M., & Mahoney, M.J. (1987). Screening for fetal Down syndrome in pregnancy by measuring maternal serum alpha-fetoprotein levels. *New England Journal of Medicine, 317,* 342–346.

Keeler-Paul, C. (1987). Real life thoughts on amniocentesis. *Down Syndrome News, 11,* 51.

Pueschel, S.M. (1987). Maternal alpha-fetoprotein screening for Down syndrome. *New England Journal of Medicine, 317,* 376–378.

Pueschel, S.M., & Goldstein, A. (1990). Genetic counseling in mental retardation. In J.L. Matson & J.A. Mulick (Eds.), *Handbook of mental retardation* (pp. 259–269). Elmsford, NY: Pergamon Press.

Wald, M.J., Cuckle, H.S., Densem, J.W., Nanchahal, K., Royston, P., Chard, T., Haddow, J.E., Knight, G.J., Palomaki, G.E., & Cannick, J.A. (1988). Maternal serum screening for Down syndrome in early pregnancy. *British Medical Journal, 297,* 883–887.

CHAPTER 7

Pueschel, S.M. (1988). Physical characteristics, chromosome analysis, and treatment approaches in Down syndrome. In C. Tingey (Ed.), *Down syndrome: A resource handbook* (pp. 3–21). Boston: College-Hill Press/Little, Brown & Co.

Pueschel, S.M., Sassaman, E.A., Scola, P.S., Thuline, H.C., Stark, A.M., & Horrobin, M. (1982). Biomedical aspects in Down syndrome. In S.M. Pueschel & J.E. Rynders (Eds.), *Down syn-*

drome: Advances in biomedicine and the behavioral sciences (pp. 169–303). Cambridge, MA: Ware Press.

CHAPTER 8

Cronk, C., Crocker, A.C., Pueschel, S.M., Shea, A.M., Zackai, E., Pickens, G., & Reed, R.B. (1988). Growth charts for children with Down syndrome: One month to eighteen years of age. *Pediatrics, 81,* 102–110.

Pueschel, S.M. (1986). New perspectives of neurodevelopmental concerns in children with Down syndrome. In R.I. Flehming & L. Stern (Eds.), *Child development and learning behavior* (pp. 301–308). Stuttgart, NY: Gustav Fischer Verlag.

Pueschel, S.M. (1987). Health concerns in persons with Down syndrome. In S.M. Pueschel, C. Tingey, J.E. Rynders, A.C. Crocker, & D.M. Crutcher (Eds.), *New perspectives on Down syndrome* (pp. 113–133). Baltimore: Paul H. Brookes Publishing Co.

Pueschel, S.M. (1988). The biology of the maturing person with Down syndrome. In S.M. Pueschel (Ed.), *The young person with Down syndrome: Transition from adolescence to adulthood* (pp. 23–34). Baltimore: Paul H. Brookes Publishing Co.

Pueschel, S.M. (1988). Facial plastic surgery for children with Down syndrome. *Developmental Medicine and Child Neurology, 30,* 540–543.

Pueschel, S.M., & Pezzullo, J.C. (1985). Thyroid dysfunction in Down syndrome. *American Journal of Diseases of Children, 139,* 636–639.

Pueschel, S.M., & Pueschel, S.R. (1987). A study of atlantoaxial instability in children with Down syndrome. *Journal of Pediatric Neurosciences, 3,* 107–116.

CHAPTER 9

Pueschel, S.M. (1987). Defining problems and exposing useless therapy for individuals with developmental disabilities. *Down Syndrome Report, 8,* 6–15.

Pueschel, S.M. (1988). Physical characteristics, chromosome analysis, and treatment approaches in Down syndrome. In C. Tingey (Ed.), *Down syndrome: A resource handbook* (pp. 3–21). Boston: College-Hill Press/Little, Brown & Co.

Pueschel, S.M., & Castree, K. (1989). Unconventional treatments for people with Down syndrome. In J.A. Mulick & R.F. Antonak (Eds.), *Transitions in mental retardation: Applications and implications of technology* (pp. 201–212). Norwood, NJ: Ablex Publishing Corp.

CHAPTER 10

Cronk, C.E. & Pueschel, S.M. (1984). Anthropometric studies. In S.M. Pueschel (Ed.), *The young child with Down syndrome* (pp. 105–141). New York: Human Sciences Press.

Cullen, S.M., Cronk, C.E., Pueschel, S.M., Schnell, R.R., & Reed, R.R. (1984). Social development and feeding milestones. In S.M. Pueschel (Ed.), *The young child with Down syndrome* (pp. 227–252). New York: Human Sciences Press.

Schnell, R.R. (1984). Psychomotor development. In S.M. Pueschel (Ed.), *The young child with Down syndrome* (pp. 207–226). New York: Human Sciences Press.

Zausmer, E., & Shea, A. (1984). Motor development. In S.M. Pueschel (Ed.), *The young child with Down syndrome* (pp. 143–206). New York: Human Sciences Press.

CHAPTER 11

Feuerstein, R., Rand, Y., & Rynders, J. (1988). *Don't accept me as I am: Helping "retarded" people to excel.* New York: Plenum Press.

Hanson, M.J. (1987). Early intervention for children with Down syndrome. In S.M. Pueschel, C. Tingey, J.E. Rynders, A.C. Crocker, & D.M. Crutcher (Eds.), *New perspectives on Down syndrome* (pp. 149–170). Baltimore: Paul H. Brookes Publishing Co.

Pueschel, S.M. (1988). *The young person with Down syndrome: Transition from adolescence to adulthood.* Baltimore: Paul H. Brookes Publishing Co.

CHAPTER 12

Hanson, M.J., & Harris, S.R. (1986). *Teaching the young child with motor delays.* Austin: PRO-ED.

Shea, A. (1987). *Motor development in Down syndrome.* Unpublished doctoral dissertation, Harvard University School of Public Health, Boston.

Tingey, C. (1988). *Down syndrome: A resource handbook.* Boston: College-Hill Press/Little, Brown & Co.

Zausmer, E., & Shea, A. (1984). Motor development. In S.M. Pueschel (Ed.), *The young child with Down syndrome* (pp. 143–206). New York: Human Sciences Press.

CHAPTER 13

Casto, G. (1989). Cognitive development. In C. Tingey (Ed.), *Implementing early intervention* (pp. 209–224). Baltimore: Paul H. Brookes Publishing Co.

Feuerstein, R., Rand, Y., Hoffmann, B., & Miller, R. (1980). *Instrumental enrichment.* Baltimore: University Park Press.

Montessori, M. (1967). *The absorbent mind.* New York: Holt, Rinehart & Winston.

Narrol, H.G., & Giblon, S.T. (1984). *Uncovering hidden learning potential.* Baltimore: University Park Press.

CHAPTER 14

Cullen, S.M. (1973). *Toward independent feeding.* Waltham, MA: New England Developmental Disabilities Communication Center.

Cullen, M., Cronk, C.E., Pueschel, S.M., Schnell, R.R., & Reed, R.B. (1984). Social development and feeding milestones. In S.M. Pueschel (Ed.), *The young child with Down syndrome* (pp. 227–252). New York: Human Sciences Press.

Good, J. (1980). *Breastfeeding the Down's syndrome baby.* Franklin Park, IL: La Leche League International.

Pueschel, S.M., Bernier, J.C., & Weidenman, L.E. (1988). *The special child* (pp. 160–161, 266–268). Baltimore: Paul H. Brookes Publishing Co.

CHAPTER 15

Pueschel, S.M., Tingey, C., Rynders, J.E., Crocker, A.C., & Crutcher, D.M. (Eds.). (1987). *New perspectives on Down syndrome.* Baltimore: Paul H. Brookes Publishing Co.
Stray-Gundersen, K. (Ed.). (1986). *Babies with Down syndrome: A new parent's guide.* Rockville, MD: Woodbine House.

CHAPTER 16

Irwin, K.C. (1989). The school achievement of children with Down's syndrome. *New Zealand Medical Journal, 102,* 11–13.
Pieterse, M., & Center, Y. (1984). The integration of eight Down's syndrome children into regular schools. *Australia and New Zealand Journal of Developmental Disabilities, 10,* 11–20.
Rynders, J.E., Spiker, D., & Horrobin, J.M. (1978). Underestimating the educability of Down's syndrome children: Examination of methodological problems in recent literature. *American Journal of Mental Deficiency, 82,* (5), 440–448.
Wilcox, B., & Bellamy, G.T. (1987). Secondary education for students with Down syndrome: Implementing quality services. In S.M. Pueschel, C. Tingey, J.E. Rynders, A.C. Crocker, & D.M. Crutcher (Eds.), *New perspectives on Down syndrome* (pp. 203–224). Baltimore: Paul H. Brookes Publishing Co.

CHAPTER 17

Egan, I., Fredericks, B., Peters, J., Hendrickson, K., Bunse, C., & Towes, J. (1984). *Teaching associated work skills: A manual.* Monmouth, OR: Teaching Research Publications.

Fredericks, H.D., & Fredericks, D.K. (1980). Batter up: Baseball for children with disabilities. *Exceptional Parent, 10,* (3), 29–30.

Fredericks, H.D., Mushlitz, J., & DeRoest, C. (1986). Integration of children with Down syndrome at the elementary school level: A pilot study. In S.M. Pueschel, C. Tingey, J.E. Rynders, A.C. Crocker, & D.M. Crutcher (Eds.), *New perspectives on Down syndrome* (pp. 179–193). Baltimore: Paul H. Brookes Publishing Co.

Hart, B. (1985). Environmental techniques that may facilitate generalization and acquisition. In S. Warren & A. Rogers–Warren (Eds.), *Functional language intervention* (pp. 145–192). Baltimore: University Park Press.

Holvoet, J., Guess, D., Mulligan, M., & Brown, F. (1980). The individualized curriculum sequencing model (II): A teaching strategy for severely handicapped students. *Journal of The Association for the Severely Handicapped, 5,* 337–351.

Horner, R.H., McDonnell, J.J., & Bellamy, G.T. (1986). Teaching generalized skills: General case instruction in simulation and community settings. In R.H. Horner, L.H. Meyer, & H.D. Fredericks (Eds.), *Education of learners with severe handicaps: Exemplary service strategies* (pp. 289–314). Baltimore: Paul H. Brookes Publishing Co.

Makohon, L., & Fredericks, H.D. (1985). *Teaching expressive and receptive language to students with moderate and severe handicaps.* Austin: PRO-ED.

Newsom, R. (1981). School. In I.O. Lovaas (Ed.), *Teaching developmentally disabled children: The me book* (pp. 223–234). Baltimore: University Park Press.

Peterson, J., Trecker, N., Egan, I., Fredericks, B., & Bunse, C. (1983). *Teaching research assessment procedures for secondary students with severe handicaps.* Monmouth, OR: Teaching Research Publications.

Sailor, W., Halvorsen, A., Anderson, J., Goetz, L., Gee, K., Doering, K., & Hunt, P. (1986). Community intensive instruction. In R.H. Horner, L.H. Meyer, & H.D. Fredericks (Eds.), *Education of learners with severe handicaps: Exemplary service strategies* (pp. 251–288). Baltimore: Paul H. Brookes Publishing Co.

Staff of the Teaching Research Infant and Child Center. (1980).

The Teaching Research Curriculum for moderately and severely handicapped (Vols. 1 & 2). Springfield, IL: Charles C Thomas.

CHAPTER 18

Baker, B.L., & Brightman, A.J. (1989). *Steps to independence.* Baltimore: Paul H. Brookes Publishing Co.

Chance, P. (1979). *Learning through play.* New York: Gardner Press.

MacDonald, W.S., & Oden, C.W. (1978). *Moose: A very special person.* Minneapolis: Winston Press.

Perske, R. (1984). *Show me no mercy.* Nashville: Abingdon Press.

Perske, R. (1988). *Circle of friends.* Nashville: Abingdon Press.

CHAPTER 19

Edginton, C.R., Compton, D.M., & Hanson, C.J. (1980). Recreation and leisure in a contemporary society. *Recreation and Leisure Programming, 6,* 3–24.

Kraus, R. (1978). Recreation and leisure today: An overview. *Recreation and Leisure in Modern Society, 5,* 2–45.

Special Olympics International. (1989). *Unified Sports handbook.*

CHAPTER 20

Broen, P. (1972). The verbal environment of the language-learning child. *American Speech and Hearing Association Monographs, 17.*

Cherry, L. (1979, September). *Theoretical bases of language and communication development in preschool children.* Paper presented at the Symposium on Developmental Disabilities in the Preschool Child: Early Identification, Assessment, and Intervention Strategies, Chicago.

Clark, H., & Clark, E. (1977). *Psychology and language.* San Diego: Harcourt, Brace, Jovanovich.

Cross, T.G. (1977). Mother's speech adjustments: The contribution of selected child listener variables. In C.E. Snow & C.A. Ferguson (Eds.), *Talking to children: Language input and acquisition* (pp. 151–183). Cambridge, MA: Cambridge University Press.

Garnica, O.K. (1975, Sept.). *Nonverbal concommitants of language input to children.* Paper presented at the Third International Child Language Symposium, London.

Horstmeier, D. (1985). *The mother-child communicative interactions of educationally advantaged Down syndrome and normal children matched for auditory comprehension.* Unpublished doctoral dissertation, Ohio State University, Columbus.

Horstmeier, D., & MacDonald, J.D. (1978). *Ready, set, go: Talk to me.* Columbus, OH: Charles E. Merrill.

Horstmeier, D., & Tingey, C. (1989). Atmosphere for language learning. In C. Tingey (Ed.), *Implementing early intervention* (pp. 167–188). Baltimore: Paul H. Brookes Publishing Co.

Iglesias, A., & Horstmeier, D. (1978, May). *Speech intelligibility training.* Paper presented at the Down Syndrome Interest Group of the American Association on Mental Deficiency Convention, Miami.

Leitch, S.M. (1977). *A child learns to speak: A guide for parents and teachers of preschool children.* Springfield, IL: Charles C Thomas.

Lombardino, L., & MacDonald, J.D. (1978). *Mother's speech acts during play interaction with nondelayed and Down syndrome children.* Unpublished doctoral dissertation, Ohio State University, Columbus.

MacDonald, J.D., & Gillette, Y. (1982). *A conversational approach to language delay: Problems and solutions.* Columbus: Ohio State University Press.

Marcell, M.M., & Armstrong, V. (1982). Auditory and visual sequential memory of Down syndrome and nonretarded children. *American Journal of Mental Deficiency, 87,* 86–95.

McCormick, L., & Schiefelbusch, R. (1984). *Early language intervention.* Columbus, OH: Charles E. Merrill.

Miller, J. (1987). Language and communication characteristics of children with Down syndrome. In S.M. Pueschel, C. Tingey,

J.E. Rynders, A.C. Crocker, & D.M. Crutcher (Eds.), *New perspectives on Down syndrome* (pp. 233–262). Baltimore: Paul H. Brookes Publishing Co.

Nelson, K. (1973). Structure and strategy in learning to talk. *Monographs of the Society for Research in Child Development, 38* (1–2, Serial No. 149).

Phillips, J. (1973). Syntax and vocabulary of mother's speech to young children: Age and sex comparisons. *Child Development, 44,* 182–185.

Rondal, J.A. (1977). Maternal speech to normal and Down's syndrome children matched for mean length of utterance. In P. Mittler (Ed.), *Research to practice in mental retardation: Vol. 2: Education and training* (pp. 239–243). Baltimore: University Park Press.

Smith, B., & Oller, K. (1981). A comparative study of pre-meaningful vocalizations produced by normally developing and Down's syndrome infants. *Journal of Speech and Hearing Research, 45,* 46–51.

Tingey, C. (1989). *Implementing early intervention.* Baltimore: Paul H. Brookes Publishing Co.

Weigel-Crum, C.A. (1981). The development of grammar in Down syndrome children between the mental ages of 2–0 and 6–11 years. *Education and Training of the Mentally Retarded, 16,* 24–30.

CHAPTER 21

Edwards, J.P. (1979). *Being me: A social-sexual training guidebook.* Austin: PRO-ED.

Edwards, J.P. (1987). Living options for persons with Down syndrome. In S. Pueschel, C. Tingey, J.E. Rynders, A.C. Crocker, & D.M. Crutcher (Eds.), *New perspectives on Down syndrome* (pp. 337–354). Baltimore: Paul H. Brookes Publishing Co.

Edwards, J.P. (1988). Sexuality, marriage, and parenting for persons with Down syndrome. In S.M. Pueschel (Ed.), *The young person with Down syndrome* (pp. 187–204). Baltimore: Paul H. Brookes Publishing Co.

Edwards, J.P. (1988). Strategies for meeting the needs of adolescents and adults. In V. Dmitriev & P. Oelwein (Eds.), *Advances in Down syndrome*. Seattle: Special Child Publications.

Edwards, J.P., & Dawson, D. (1983). *My friend David. A source book about Down syndrome* (pp. 101–118). Austin: PRO-ED.

Edwards, J.P., & Elkins, T.E. (1988). *Just between us. A social sexual guide for parents and professionals with concerns for persons with developmental disabilities* (pp. 43–53, 55, 77–98, 115–117). Austin: PRO-ED.

Elkins, T.E., Rosen, D., Heaton, C., Sorg, C., Kope, S., McNeeley, S.G., & DeLancey, J.O. (1988). A program to accomplish pelvic exams in difficult to manage patients with mental retardation. *Adolescent and Pediatric Gynecology, 1* (3), 185–188.

Frank, R., & Edwards, J.E. (1988). *Building self-esteem in persons with developmental disabilities*. Austin: PRO-ED.

Perske, R. (1988). *Circle of friends*. Nashville: Abingdon Press.

CHAPTER 22

Edwards, J.P. (1976). *Sara and Allen: The right to choose*. Portland: Ednick Communications.

Edwards, J.P., & Elkins, T.E. (1988). *Just between us*. Portland: Ednick Communications.

CHAPTER 23

Fifield, M., & Smith, B. (1985). *Personnel training*. Technical Report 5. Logan: Utah State University Affiliated Facility, Developmental Center for Handicapped Persons.

Karan, O.C., Knight, C.B., & Pauls, D. (1987). Vocational opportunities: An exploration of the issues. In S.M. Pueschel, C. Tingey, J.E. Rynders, A.C. Crocker, & D.M. Crutcher (Eds.), *New perspectives on Down syndrome* (pp. 355–377). Baltimore: Paul H. Brookes Publishing Co.

Kiernan, B., & Stark, J. (1985). *Employment options.* Technical Report 2. Logan: Utah State University Affiliated Facility, Developmental Center for Handicapped Persons.

Lane, D. (1985). After school: Work and employment for adults with Down's syndrome? In D. Lane & B. Stratford (Eds.), *Current approaches to Down's syndrome* (pp. 386–400). Westport, CT: Greenwood Press.

CHAPTER 24

Close, D.W., & Keating, T.J. (1988). Toward independent living. In S.M. Pueschel (Ed.), *The young person with Down syndrome* (pp. 173–185). Baltimore: Paul H. Brookes Publishing Co.

Edwards, J. (1987). Living options for persons with Down syndrome. In S.M. Pueschel, C. Tingey, J.E. Rynders, A.C. Crocker, & D.M. Crutcher (Eds.), *New perspectives on Down syndrome* (pp. 337–354). Baltimore: Paul H. Brookes Publishing Co.

Index